Bat

Animal
Series editor: Jonathan Burt

Already published

Albatross Graham Barwell · *Ant* Charlotte Sleigh · *Ape* John Sorenson · *Badger* Daniel Heath Justice
Bat Tessa Laird · *Bear* Robert E. Bieder · *Beaver* Rachel Poliquin · *Bee* Claire Preston · *Beetle* Adam Dodd
Bison Desmond Morris · *Camel* Robert Irwin · *Cat* Katharine M. Rogers · *Chicken* Annie Potts
Cockroach Marion Copeland · *Cow* Hannah Velten · *Crocodile* Dan Wylie · *Crow* Boria Sax
Deer John Fletcher · *Dog* Susan McHugh · *Dolphin* Alan Rauch · *Donkey* Jill Bough
Duck Victoria de Rijke · *Eagle* Janine Rogers · *Eel* Richard Schweid · *Elephant* Dan Wylie
Falcon Helen Macdonald · *Flamingo* Caitlin R. Kight · *Fly* Steven Connor · *Fox* Martin Wallen
Frog Charlotte Sleigh · *Giraffe* Edgar Williams · *Goat* Joy Hinson · *Gorilla* Ted Gott and
Kathryn Weir · *Guinea Pig* Dorothy Yamamoto · *Hare* Simon Carnell · *Hedgehog* Hugh Warwick
Hippopotamus Edgar Williams · *Horse* Elaine Walker · *Hyena* Mikita Brottman · *Kangaroo* John Simons
Leech Robert G. W. Kirk and Neil Pemberton · *Leopard* Desmond Morris · *Lion* Deirdre Jackson
Lizard Boria Sax · *Llama* Helen Cowie · *Lobster* Richard J. King · *Monkey* Desmond Morris
Moose Kevin Jackson · *Mosquito* Richard Jones · *Moth* Matthew Gandy · *Mouse* Georgie Carroll
Octopus Richard Schweid · *Ostrich* Edgar Williams · *Otter* Daniel Allen · *Owl* Desmond Morris
Oyster Rebecca Stott · *Parrot* Paul Carter · *Peacock* Christine E. Jackson · *Penguin* Stephen Martin
Pig Brett Mizelle · *Pigeon* Barbara Allen · *Rabbit* Victoria Dickenson · *Rat* Jonathan Burt
Rhinoceros Kelly Enright · *Salmon* Peter Coates · *Scorpion* Louise M. Pryke · *Seal* Victoria Dickenson
Shark Dean Crawford · *Sheep* Philip Armstrong · *Skunk* Alyce Miller · *Snail* Peter Williams
Snake Drake Stutesman · *Sparrow* Kim Todd · *Spider* Katarzyna and Sergiusz Michalski
Swallow Angela Turner · *Swan* Peter Young · *Tiger* Susie Green · *Tortoise* Peter Young
Trout James Owen · *Vulture* Thom van Dooren · *Walrus* John Miller and Louise Miller
Whale Joe Roman · *Wild Boar* Dorothy Yamamoto · *Wolf* Garry Marvin · *Woodpecker* Gerard Gorman
Zebra Christopher Plumb and Samuel Shaw

Bat

Tessa Laird

REAKTION BOOKS

For Ninja, the beautiful black bat-cat, RIP

Published by
REAKTION BOOKS LTD
Unit 32, Waterside
44–48 Wharf Road
London N1 7UX, UK
www.reaktionbooks.co.uk

First published 2018
Copyright © Tessa Laird 2018

Printed and bound in China by 1010 Printing International Ltd

A catalogue record for this book is available from the British Library

ISBN 9 781 78023 894 4

Contents

1 Dazzling Diversity: The Biology of Chiroptera

The scientific classification for bats is Chiroptera, and it is one of the most diverse orders of mammalia on the planet, comprising over 1,331 species.[1] Rodents are the only mammalian order boasting more species than bats, but they are arguably less thrilling than their winged cousins, who range from monster-sized fruit eaters with a wingspan the length of an adult human to tiny insectivores weighing little more than a bumblebee. The success of such diverse chiropterans can be attributed to evolutionary developments dating back more than 50 million years, the most obvious being that bats are the only mammals that are capable of true flight. Additionally, most bats can echolocate, emitting high-pitched sonic pulses whose echoes they interpret to build up a picture of their surroundings and their prey.[2] These, along with several other 'superpowers', demonstrate not only the dazzling diversity of Chiroptera but their intrinsic role in the maintenance of healthy ecosystems. Such mysterious powers may also offer a clue as to why bats are so commonly feared. Their association with evil, magic and madness finds them most often in the company of filmic and literary villains. Occasionally, however, their superpowers inspire superheroes.

The habitats, diets and physical characteristics of bats differ so vastly that Richard Dawkins said that to speak of bats as though they were all the same would be 'to speak of dogs, lions, weasels,

Two grey-headed flying foxes hanging out together.

7

Some of the first known images of bats can be found in the ancient Egyptian tomb paintings at Beni Hasan, Twelfth Dynasty, about 2000 BCE. Here a bat with wings spread wide can just be made out beneath a palimpsest of hieroglyphs and Coptic inscriptions.

bears, hyenas, pandas and otters all in one breath, just because they are all carnivores'.[3] Yet bats persist in the popular imagination as a rather generic type: small, black, squeaky and leathery. They are largely ignored except for their regular appearances in Halloween decorations, horror films and virus outbreaks. Meanwhile, climate change and habitat loss are depleting global bat populations at an alarming rate, making it more important than ever that we understand the biology and behaviour of these fascinating and varied creatures. As the great American modernist poet Marianne Moore put it, when describing a bat, 'we / do not admire what / we cannot understand'.[4]

Chiroptera is a compound of two Greek words, *chier* meaning hand and *pteron* meaning wing. Bats have very short upper arms while their forearms are greatly elongated, their fingers even more so. Each 'spoke' of their webbed wings (which somewhat resemble black umbrellas) is actually a finger, and the tiny hook at the top of each wing is equivalent to a human thumb. Recent research emphasizes the sensitivity of bats' wings, which, like human hands, are full of sensory receptors. This sense of touch makes bats' wings superbly adapted for flight, but they can equally be used to scoop insects or cradle a baby.[5] Bats also use their leathery appendages as raincoats or sleeping bags; many bats sleep hanging upside down from trees, wrapped in their own wings. Bats' legs, however, are comparatively short and stumpy, and their clawed feet resemble our hands. They use these claws like grappling hooks (one of Batman's favourite tools) with which to hang upside down without effort – attested to by the fact that dead bats are often found still dangling by a vice-like grip. A fruit bat can hang comfortably from one leg, and looks in this posture like a piece of furry fruit, a veritable 'animated pear', as one bat researcher put it.[6] As if constant inversion wasn't strange enough, bats are unique among mammals for having knees that point outwards rather than forwards, an attribute that facilitates steering during flight and helps them crawl across surfaces such as the interiors of caves. In this posture, they look something like giant furry crickets.

For a long time the order Chiroptera was divided into two suborders: Microchiroptera and Megachiroptera, often simply called microbats and megabats, or, in German, the dainty *Fledermaus* versus the hefty *Flughund*. While the two suborders have been recently revised, they are still useful for distinguishing broadly between two very different types of bat. The former are

Unknown artist, detail from the Aberdeen Bestiary, c. 1200, folio 51v.

Centurio senex, or
wrinkle-faced bat,
from Belize.

predominantly small insect-eaters who use echolocation for
navigation, and comprise a vast array of species with bizarre,
fleshy facial ornaments, which the eighteenth-century French
naturalist the Comte de Buffon described as 'a kind of pudding
above the lips'.[7] (Perhaps this says more about the comestibles
of Buffon's era than it does about bats' faces.) The latter are the
larger fruit-eaters whose common name 'flying fox' gives a good
indication of their endearingly dog-like faces, with large eyes,
twitching ears, long snouts and lolling tongues. These fruit bats
are restricted to mostly tropical regions – Africa, parts of Asia
and Indo-Australasia – and constitute a single family, the Pteropodidae. Microbats, on the other hand, can be found on every
continent except Antarctica, and comprise eighteen different
families.[8] In order to cope with a vast range of climatic conditions,
bats that live in colder locations have developed the ability to

hibernate; in hibernation their hearts, which run to around 400 beats per minute while awake, drop to a mere 25 beats.[9]

Even those living in warmer climates can use torpor, a drop in body temperature and metabolic rate, as a flexible energy-saving strategy, not unlike a hybrid car.[10] Nevertheless, the vast majority (over 80 per cent) of all bat species live in tropical climes, leading biologists to suspect that bats evolved in tropical regions.[11]

A recent reclassification of bats, still in two camps, uses modern genetic sequencing and puts some of the microbats into the mega category, now known as Yinpterochiroptera, while the rest of the microbats are accounted for under the subordinal heading of Yangochiroptera. That this system recalls the Chinese symbol of yin-yang – opposites that mingle and flux – is apposite given the Chinese love of bats as being symbolic of good luck. The newly delineated categories contain a big surprise: the superfamily Rhinolophoidea, which includes horseshoe bats, leaf-nosed bats and ghost bats, is more closely related to the Pteropodidae or fruit bat family than to microbats. This is remarkable because the Rhinolophoidea are the most complex and sophisticated echo-locators – they are able to alter their calls subtly to compensate for error due to the Doppler effect, that is, the changing frequencies caused by the shifting positions of both predator and prey – while most flying foxes don't echolocate at all.[12]

Up until 2008 a controversy raged among evolutionary biologists as to whether flying foxes shared any common ancestry with echolocating microbats. The Australian neuroscientist Jack Pettigrew argued against bat monophyly (descent from a single common ancestor) and promoted the idea of convergent evolution – two separate groups of mammals that evolved flight independently of each other. He even went so far as to suggest that flying foxes were descended from a kind of 'flying primate'. Pettigrew deployed many compelling arguments to prove his point, including aspects of the flying foxes' reproductive cycle. For example, foraging microbats leave their young at home in communal 'nurseries', while megabats carry their young with them just as primates do.[13] Megabats have a recognizable menstrual cycle, which is a feature common to primates, and extraordinarily uncommon in the vast majority of all other animal species. Defecation also provides clues: fruit bats reverse position, dangling upright by their hooked 'thumbs' (as does the colugo, a gliding mammal from Southeast Asia, to which Pettigrew believed that fruit bats were connected). In contrast, microbats defecate while dangling upside down, and simply arch their backs to avoid soiling their fur.[14] But the key piece of evidence that started Pettigrew on his voyage of discovery in the first place is that megabats' eyes, as well as the wiring of their optic nerves, conform to the primate model and are totally different to those of microbats.[15]

Pettigrew's hypothesis was always speculative, and he himself said, perhaps in honour of his frugivorous subjects, that even if proven wrong, it would remain a 'most fruitful, wrong hypothesis'.[16] DNA experiments ultimately appeared to disprove Pettigrew's hypothesis, but led to the new 'yin-yang' system of classification. The current consensus is that bats *are* monophyletic, that is, descended from a common ancestor, and that megabats evolved from microbats, although gaps in the fossil record have had some scientists argue that the reverse might be the case. In a rather fruity train of thought, Glover Morrill Allen, an American zoologist working in the early twentieth century, pondered whether vampire bats might first have been fruit-juice drinkers who later learned to puncture the skins of animals 'to secure their juices'.[17] The prevailing scientific thinking, however, suggests that fruit-eating megabats were indeed descended from echolocating, insect-eating microbats. Not only have megabats lost the ability to echolocate, but they have lost the very anatomy required to do so.[18] It may be that echolocation limits the size of bats, since calls are coupled to respiratory and wingbeat cycles. As bats get bigger and wingbeat frequency drops, call emission frequency also falls, and this would reduce the rate of information reception, making it a less viable option for larger bats, although *Vampyrum spectrum*, with a wingspan of nearly 1 metre, manages to echolocate despite its large size.[19]

Whatever the scientific truth, Pettigrew's opinion that 'some bats are much less like mice or birds than they are like people' allows for a charmingly empathetic engagement with a group of animals that have hitherto been thought of as bestial, devilish and 'other'.[20] Pettigrew even included something he called the 'fallen angel' hypothesis in his theory of convergent evolution, 'for poetic and logical completeness only', in which winged primates evolve first, but later some branches of the family lose their airborne appendages.[21] Taking this hypothesis to its 'poetic and logical' extreme would make us humans a kind of 'flightless bat'.

Genetic relationships between humans and bats may sound far-fetched, but in parts of Australia and Papua New Guinea kinship between these two groups is revered in myths and song cycles. Even the great eighteenth-century taxonomist Carl von Linnaeus placed bats close to humans in his first attempt at an evolutionary

Spectre Bat

'Spectre Bat', now known as the spectral bat or *Vampyrum spectrum*, in J. Johnson's *The Natural History of Quadrupeds (after Linnaeus)* (1801). The mammal's mammaries are rather prominent, following Linnaeus's coinage of the class of Mammalia after the Latin word for breast.

Ectophylla alba, Honduran white bats, making their home in a leaf tent in Costa Rica. The bats have cut the midribs of the leaf to form a tent.

classification system, noting that only primates, elephants and bats possess a single pair of nipples for suckling their young.[22] Linnaeus coined the name of the entire class of mammalia from the Latin word for 'breast', since mammals are all suckled on their mothers' milk. It was Linnaeus' focus on the breasts of mammals (rather than his later categorization by teeth) which had us briefly occupy the same taxonomic category as the bat. As one author put it, Linnaeus had been 'led astray by the location of the mammae', as many good men have been, before and since.[23]

To be fair, however, it is bats' differences from us, and from each other, that make them such a fascinating subject. There are tiny, furry white bats, with yellow ears and noses, that curl up in fluffy balls in 'tents' they fashion from folded leaves in the tropical forests of Honduras and Costa Rica. *Kerivoula picta*, the painted bat, is apricot buff with orange and black wings in a fetching zigzag known as 'cryptic' patterning, so the creature can pass as a withered leaf as it hangs quietly in Asian woodlands. In 1896 the appropriately named Major S. S. Flower reported from Thailand (then Siam) that he had found a specimen of this beautiful bat

The *Kerivoula picta* is also known as the painted bat, or butterfly bat, due to its striking markings and fluttering flight. This Southeast Asian bat is safely camouflaged as it roosts among dry leaves.

The habitat of *Euderma maculatum*, or spotted bat, ranges from the Grand Canyon in Arizona to parts of Canada.

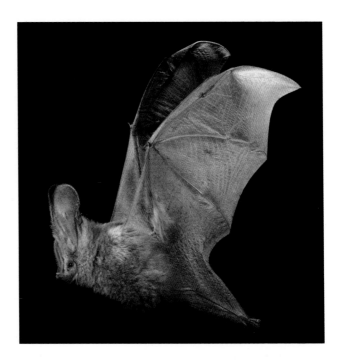

Lavia frons in flight. This golden-winged bat from Kenya often roosts in bushes with yellowish orange berries; otherwise its remarkably colourful flight equipment remains a mystery.

curled up in a calla lily.[24] Henry David Thoreau wrote of finding a tiny red bat hanging asleep among some ferns, and compared its rusty brown fur to the cinnamon-coloured 'wool' of the fern, as well as the 'plush of a ripe cat-tail head'.[25] The butterfly bat of Cameroon has delicately veined wings that resemble a skeleton-ized leaf. The spotted bat sports a black back with three white circles making a kind of face, less a death's head than a 'surprise' emoticon. This bat roosts in the Grand Canyon, and has the longest ears of any bat for its body size. The African yellow-winged bat possesses, as you might have guessed, yellow wings, as well as silvery-white fur and dramatic ears which look as if two enormous gold-plated cockroaches have burrowed into the bat's brow.

Together with its sharp, triangular nose, this bat looks every bit an emissary from outer space.

The giant golden-crowned flying fox of the Philippines is one of the largest of the megabats, reaching a wingspan of almost 180 cm, and weighing over a kilogram. These beautiful endangered creatures are hunted both for meat and for their pelts. At the other end of the scale, the lesser bamboo bat, found in South and Southeast Asia, is so diminutive that it can hide inside the hollow stems of bamboo, using tiny adhesive pads to grip the smooth interior surface. Another tiny sucker-footed bat called *Myzopoda* is found only in Madagascar; with a wise face and extravagant, upswept ears, it resembles a little brown Yoda (although the prize for looking most like Yoda, which is fiercely contested in the bat kingdom, might rather be bestowed upon the nyctimene tube-nosed fruit bat of Papua New Guinea). The smallest chiropteran of all is Kitti's hog-nosed bat of Thailand, the so-called bumblebee bat, which weighs just 2 grams. Arguably the smallest mammal on the planet, this bat is sadly vulnerable owing to habitat loss.

A list of types of bat is a veritable cascade of evolutionary variety: there are bats whose names suggest they have noses shaped like leaves, swords, horseshoes, tridents and spears. There are not

One of the largest of the megabats, *Acerodon jubatus*, the golden-crowned flying fox of the Philippines.

The smallest bat of all and possibly the world's smallest mammal, *Craseonycteris thonglongyai* or Kitti's hog-nosed bat.

just leaf-*nosed* bats, but leaf-*lipped* bats and leaf-*chinned* bats too; there are pallid bats, and African slit-faced bats (both of which feed on scorpions); there are well-dressed moustachioed bats and epauletted bats, and less appropriately attired naked-backed bats. There are spectral bats, ghost-faced bats and smoky bats. There are long-tongued, long-nosed and long-legged bats. There are not just flying foxes but bulldog bats and mastiff bats (although it is the wrinkle-faced bat who looks most like a squashed-nose pug). There are mouse-tailed bats, frog-eating bats, big-eared bats and little big-eared bats. There are woolly false vampire bats who, as their name suggests, don't actually feed on blood, and there are hairy-legged vampire bats who do. Perhaps the most effusive ode to the dazzling diversity of bats has been written by the author and naturalist Diane Ackerman, who lists a veritable 'carnival of bats' in her essay 'In Praise of Bats'. She notes that the tube-nosed fruit bats' elongated nostrils look 'like party favours' and the funnel-eared bat resembles 'a golden Pekingese', while the Brazilian free-tailed bat possesses a face 'as wrinkled as a wise old extraterrestrial's might be'.[26]

There are bats that eat fish and hunt on the wing, sometimes skimming the surface of the water, and sometimes using their wings as oars as they submerge all but their heads. In New Zealand, bats are the only native land mammal and, having gone to all the evolutionary trouble of growing wings, they spend most of their time rummaging on the forest floor, using their elbows as legs. So unique and specialized is *Mystacina tuberculata* that it possesses its own personalized species of blind, wingless bat-fly, which feeds on the fungi that grow on the bat's guano (all other species of bat-fly are parasitic, feeding on their hosts' blood).[27] The New Zealand short-tail bat's closest living relative is actually the fisherman bat of South America, an example of the separation of related families in the break-up of the Gondwanaland supercontinent in the late Cretaceous era.[28] Through the fish-eaters, the insectivorous New Zealand short-tail is a distant cousin of the only other ground-crawling bat in the world: the fearsome vampire, which creeps up on its unsuspecting prey, and can also jump several times its own length by pushing downwards with its folded wings and hind feet.[29]

The vast majority of bats, however, are insect eaters, and some species are so adept that they can catch over a thousand mosquitoes or other undesirable insects in an hour. Insectivorous bats are usually classified as either 'gleaners' that echolocate softly in order to pluck their prey from foliage, or 'aerial-hawkers' whose much louder calls enable them to catch insects on the wing – otherwise differentiated as 'whisperers' and 'screamers'.[30]

Fruit-eating bats prove to be just as pivotal to healthy ecosystems as insect-eating bats, since they pollinate and disperse the seeds of beneficial plant species. The fragrant white flowers of Arizona's iconic organ pipe and saguaro cacti are sturdy enough to bear the weight of the bats who nose-dive the blooms by night, to emerge ghost-faced, as if dusted with icing sugar. Without bats to pollinate them, these cacti could become extinct. Many tropical fruits, such as mangoes, bananas and guavas, rely on bats for either

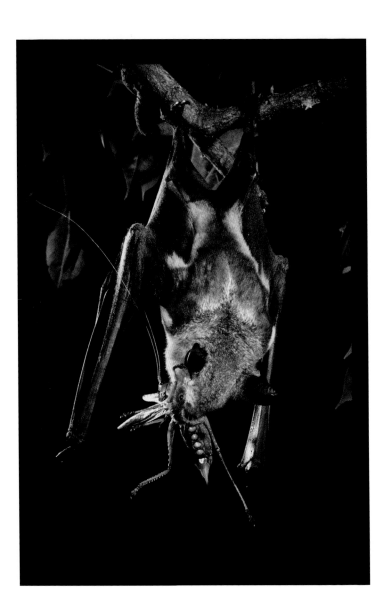

Leptonycteris curasoae, the lesser long-nosed bat, pollinating a saguaro cactus flower in Mexico.

pollination or seed dispersal in the wild, as does that notoriously odoriferous delicacy, the durian. Ackerman's sensuous description of bats among moonlit flowers imagines them as libidinous creatures, 'garish and available as prostitutes leaning against a streetlamp'. The co-evolved flowers have 'seductive, trumpetlike mouths' while the pollinating bat possesses a 'long, nectar-loving tongue'.[31] Indeed, the tube-lipped nectar bat of Ecuador has a tongue which, at 8.5 cm in length, is one and a half times longer than its entire body.

Bats' successful adaptations as hunters and foragers rely on one important factor – flight – and because they are nocturnal, they fulfil specific ecological niches that diurnal birds cannot. For example, rainforest birds avoid flying in open areas to avoid hawk attacks, whereas tropical fruit-eating bats cross great distances at night, passing seeds as they go. This makes bats the most valuable asset in terms of reforestation of cleared areas throughout the world's tropics.[32]

Hipposideros vittatus, or striped leaf-nosed bat, eats a katydid in Kenya.

23

Pteropus mariannus, Mariana flying fox, pollinating a coral tree in Guam.

With scientific understatement, the University of Leeds professor of animal ecology and dedicated bat champion John Altringham notes that 'Flying is not easy.'[33] Leonardo da Vinci, the Wright Brothers and Harry Potter would surely agree. But bats have been perfecting this, their most striking superpower, for millions of years. A distinction is made between 'true' flight and gliding, since several species of mammal have the ability to glide among tree tops thanks to a membrane between their front and back limbs. These animals cannot, however, take off from the ground, maintain altitude or stay aloft for more than a few moments, compared with the ten to twelve hours of non-stop flight which has been observed in Brazilian free-tailed bats,[34] along with prodigiously rapid wingbeats, up to twenty per second in some species.[35] Bats can migrate over distances of at least 800–1,000 km to ensure access to food sources over changing seasons.

In spite of these extraordinary feats, the Comte de Buffon, who didn't like bats' faces and didn't think much of their flying skills either, wrote: 'Their motion in the air is rather a desultory fluttering, than flying, which they execute very aukwardly.'[36] What he interpreted as erratic movement is more likely to have been the exceptionally accurate aerial acrobatics of bats hunting insects on the wing. Not only do bats possess true powered flight, but they can fly at incredible speeds through dense thickets of trees, turning tight corners again and again.[37] Donald Griffin, who discovered echolocation in bats around the time of the Second World War, wrote that the dexterity of the smaller bats, if scaled up to the dimensions of an airplane, 'would terrify even the hottest pilot'.[38]

Illustration from W. F. Kirby, *Natural History of the Animal Kingdom for the Use of Young People* (1889).

Leonardo da Vinci's design for a flying machine, Codex Atlanticus f.858r, c. 1490.

Indeed, the famous 'trench run' sequence of the original 1977 *Star Wars* film (the Rebel X-wings' attempt to detonate the Death Star while being pursued by the Empire's TIE fighters) would be a breeze for your average microbat. Unsurprisingly, in this space-age epic, it is the baddies' aircrafts – the TIE fighters – that most resemble the silhouette of a bat in flight: the advanced models are even called 'bent-wing' just like a species of bat. And who is Darth Vader, with his black cloak and bat-like face, if not a space-age Dracula?

Bats offer a different model for aerodynamics because, unlike birds, they can move their wings independently and, by folding one wing, can make rapid turns.[39] Current research involves careful analysis of bat flight in order to envisage high-tech small aircraft for the future.[40] Over five hundred years ago, Leonardo da Vinci drew countless sketches for potential flying machines which featured bat-like, rather than bird-like, wings, in which spokes or 'fingers' within the wings would allow for greater control of wing shape and thus more manoeuvrability. He recommended that flying machines imitate bats, with their flexible, super-light bones and highly elastic wings, writing in his notebook: 'Dissect the bat, and concentrate on this, and on this model arrange the machine.'[41] More than four hundred years later, in 1890, a French inventor named Clément Ader claimed he achieved manned, powered flight, albeit unsustained and uncontrolled, for 50 m, in an aircraft that looked like a large, ungainly bat.[42] This steam-powered bat-plane was criticized for its bewildering complexity of wing-movements, which 'no mortal pilot could have survived more than a few seconds.'[43] Ader's insistence on perfecting his ungainly bat-like craft long after viable aeroplanes took to the skies branded him a romantic out of tune with progressive thinking, but recent research trends may yet prove that he and Leonardo were right after all.

Clément Ader's bat-like *Avion III*, 1897, aloft in the Musée des Arts et Métiers in Paris.

Bats' wing membranes are comprised of two layers of skin sandwiching a thin layer of connective tissue and muscle fibres.[44] Like human skin, this membrane is self-repairing, so bats with wings shredded by cats or barbed-wire fences can be nursed back to health and released back into the wild. Even when at rest, bats' wings are marvels of design. Donald Griffin, who wrote *Listening in the Dark* about his discovery of echolocation in bats, observed that when folded, wings do not form large flaps like curtains, but that in fact the wing's surface turns itself into countless tiny crescent-shaped pockets which, rather fetchingly, 'fold individually like the petals of a flower'.[45]

Another stunning bat superpower is echolocation, a complex navigation system made from the sound waves bats produce with

Depiction of echolocation or bat 'sonar' by Simon Crowhurst from the Department of Earth Sciences at the University of Cambridge.

their vocal chords in the same way we speak, only at a much higher frequency.[46] These sound waves can vary in duration from 0.3 to 300 milliseconds, and are produced up to two hundred times per second and in frequencies ranging from 8 to 210 kiloherz.[47] The bat interprets the returning echoes of these sound waves in order to build up a picture of its environment. Bats are not the only animals to use echolocation – cetaceans and cave-nesting birds do too – but some species of bat have developed echolocation to an exceptional degree of sophistication. The ancestors of bats, like some mammalian insectivores today, probably emitted ultrasonic sounds and might have possessed a simple form of echolocation. It is generally assumed that bats evolved from a small nocturnal and arboreal mammal approximately 65 million years ago, although this 'proto-bat' has yet to be identified in the fossil record. The oldest fossils of true bats have been found in Wyoming and are around 50 million years old. One of these fossils, *Icaronycteris index*, is much like a modern insectivorous bat: an enlarged cochlea (a spiral-shaped cavity in the inner ear) shows that it possessed the ability to echolocate. Another fossil of the same age, however, *Onychonycteris finneyi*, is a more primitive bat, still possessing claws at the end of each of its shorter finger bones. This bat didn't have an enlarged cochlea, so was probably not an echolocator. The temporal coexistence of these two very different specimens poses interesting questions about the sequence of events in the evolution of bats.

Echolocation would have become increasingly complex as bats became more agile flyers and entered into a co-evolutionary arms race with their prey. Insects developed their own ability to hear bats' echolocation calls, and so both hunter and hunted evolved ways to outmanoeuvre the other. Some competitive species of bat even evolved 'jamming' calls, not to confuse prey but to outfox batty brethren who became rivals at dinnertime. When these calls

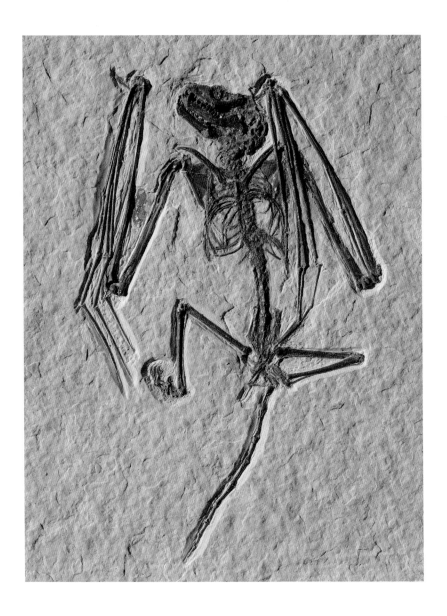

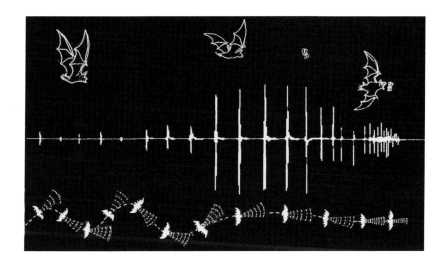

are translated into scientific imaging apparatus, they look very different from the ordered strokes on the oscilloscope which normal echolocation creates. Instead they resemble loops of telephone wire and sound something like sirens.[48] To avoid deafening themselves with their own calls, bats have specially insulated cochleas, and some species even have the ability to switch a kind of 'deafness' on and off at the same speed as their pulsing calls.[49] There are species able to shut out other bats' calls via a 'neural gate' which acts as a filter, while others possess their own personal call frequency.[50]

Like their flight techniques, bats developed their acoustic location technologies millions of years before *Homo sapiens*. An early form of human sonar was trialled in 1906 in order to map space underwater and thus detect icebergs, although clearly its application was not widespread: the *Titanic* disaster occurred in 1912. During the First World War, sonar technology was developed in order to detect enemy submarines; today we can map a

This drawing demonstrates the flight path of a common pipistrelle bat (*Pipistrellus pipistrellus*) as it hunts a moth using echolocation, with changes in pitch and frequency as the bat homes in on its prey.

Icaronycteris index, an echolocating bat that lived approximately 52 million years ago. This fossil was found in the Rocky Mountain region of the United States.

human foetus in the womb. Radar, which bounces radiowaves off objects in order to determine everything from aircraft positions to meteorology (and has even been used to track the positions of bats themselves), was conceived and developed by a range of scientists and engineers working internationally and finally patented in Britain in 1935 as a system for air defence. Neither radar nor sonar, however, was inspired by bat physiology, since Donald Griffin did not confirm echolocation in bats until 1938.

Griffin's studies represented a major breakthrough, as bats' uncanny ability to navigate in the dark had perplexed scientists for centuries. The popular misnomer 'blind as a bat' probably came about because observers such as the Comte de Buffon interpreted bat flight as erratic, but only five years after Buffon's death, in 1793, the Italian biologist and Catholic priest Lazzaro Spallanzani made a startling discovery about bats' navigational skills. Unfortunately, he killed hundreds of bats in the course of his experiments, which included blinding the poor creatures with hot needles and seeing if they could still fly. They could, and this drove Spallanzani crazy as he tried to figure out what, if anything, would 'blind' the bats, including filling their mouths and ears with glue. These tests were inconclusive, while Spallanzani's contemporary Louis Jurine of Geneva achieved better success by plugging his bats' ears with dense starch. Only then did the bats exhibit signs of 'blindness'.[51] At the time, neither scientist was able to interpret these sensory data, and for more than a century their experiments were forgotten.

In 1908 the American zoologist W. L. Hahn also discovered that tightly plugging the ears of bats caused total disorientation, and concluded that 'obstacles are perceived chiefly through sense organs in the inner ear.'[52] While his hunch was correct, neither Hahn nor any other scientist of the early twentieth century could hear the bats making noises, and so the idea of echolocation was slow to emerge. Allen, who wrote a compendium on bat biology in 1939, was aware that bats were detecting echoes reflected from objects and moving insects, but had no idea that the bats themselves were emitting high-frequency sound waves.[53] Ironically, as Allen was writing his book, Harvard undergraduate Donald Griffin had just discovered that bats produce sounds above the range of human hearing.[54] Scientists initially advanced the theory that bats might be emitting low-frequency sounds, later revising this idea to the more plausible high-frequency range. It was not until the Second World War that a sufficiently sophisticated apparatus was developed to detect sound waves above the frequency range of human hearing. Confirmation ensued: bats were indeed emitting a constant stream of sounds. Initially, it was thought that echolocation was used only to navigate, and it took some years to realize that it served a dual function as a hunting tool.

While humans require external hardware – machines that go *ping* – to map space with ultrasonic frequencies, bats do it all via intricate internal sensory systems, including their enlarged cochlea, and in many cases, an external tragus, a cartilaginous projection at the base of the ear which operates as a kind of receiver. Those bats that have developed noseleaves echolocate through their noses rather than their mouths. The leafy protuberance serves as an acoustic lens which focuses the nasally emitted echolocation pulses, allowing the bat to simultaneously eat or drink.[55] Calls are usually synched to wingbeats, increasing in speed as bats home in on prey, with different sizes of insects requiring different frequencies. Some bats even use harmonics, like Tibetan throat singers, creating sympathetic vibrations that increase the complexity of information the bat receives, turning hunting into a high art form.[56]

Echolocation isn't only used for guidance or catching insects. Some bats echolocate to recognize the unique petal shapes of specific nectar-bearing flowers.[57] The neotropical vine *Mucuna holtonii*, which has co-evolved with echolocating bats, has a concave petal which stands erect and acts as an acoustic mirror for reflecting a bat's calls.[58] And while bats are definitively not blind, different species possess different capabilities when it comes to visual range. All bats have well-developed rod photoreceptors for night vision, and, while it was previously assumed that bats had no cone photoreceptors (those needed for daylight and colour vision) at all, many bat species show one or two types of cones (humans possess three), thus the range of vision of Chiroptera is broader than once thought.[59] Bats that hunt for night-blooming flowers are sensitive to the ultraviolet spectrum, which humans can't see at all. Even those bats that don't see colour are finely tuned to spectral changes in the echoes bouncing off moving targets. Biologist John Altringham describes the way bats might perceive such phenomena metaphorically, as 'a change in the colour composition', emphasizing the complexity and artistry of bat senses.[60]

Herein lies a paradox for bat fanciers. One of bats' key attractions is their air of mystery, as they dart, black-clad and ninja-like, in and out of the shadows. And yet, the bats themselves live in a world of constant commotion. Naturalist, illustrator and author Russell Peterson called his charming and witty 1964 handbook of bats *Silently, by Night*, but he admitted in his preface that the title was erroneous, because 'bats are actually shouting their heads off'.[61] Diane Ackerman finds this an eerie thought as she stands in a 'seemingly silent' bat-filled grove, nevertheless pondering that bats 'spend their whole lives yelling at the world and each other. They yell at their loved ones, they yell at their enemies, they yell at their dinner, they yell at the big bustling world. Some yell fast, some slow, some loud, some soft.'[62] In *The Blind Watchmaker*, Richard Dawkins considers our inability to hear bats'

calls fortunate, as they would be deafeningly loud and impossible to sleep through.[63] Every bat has its own unique signature call, but if humans want to be privy to this vocalizing, they have to resort to 'bat detectors', which reduce the frequencies of bat calls so that they are within the audible range for humans. Translating the very noisy worlds of supposedly stealthy creatures for human ears, bat detectors emit sounds something like those of a Geiger counter or, in moments of batty excitement, a string of firecrackers exploding.

Surprisingly for these fast-moving, fast-talking animals, bats are the slowest-reproducing mammals in the world for their body size. Relatively speaking, they have a slow development to sexual maturity and long pregnancies, with most species producing only

The tiny Hardwicke's woolly bat, *Kerivoula hardwickii,* can be found roosting in pitcher plants in Borneo. In this co-evolutionary arrangement, the plant offers the bat shelter while it feeds on nitrogen from the bat's droppings. The bat gets a handy bedside commode, but must be sure to stay above the pitcher's digestive juices.

Grey-headed flying
fox with young in
New South Wales,
Australia.

one young annually, although occasionally twins, and even quadruplets, occur. Unfortunately for mother bats, young can range from 25 to 30 per cent of the mother's body weight.[64] The slow breeding of bats is compensated for by their long lifespans: they are the longest-lived mammals for their size, frequently achieving ages of between twenty and thirty years, while the lifespan of the Brandt's myotis, a common vesper bat of Europe and Asia, can exceed forty years.[65]

Because of the wide diversity in bat species, there are all kinds of approaches to mating and reproduction. There are bats that are all-out promiscuous, bats that are monogamous and bats that are polygynous, having more than one 'wife' at a time. Cory Toth, a researcher of *Mystacina tuberculata*, New Zealand's lesser short-tailed bat, claimed to have witnessed a batty 'threesome' but was too much of a gentleman to divulge the details.[66] He did note, however, that the short-tailed bats have a 'lekking' system, where males perform to attract passing females by singing and wearing 'aftershave' made of their own urine. Some males sing their hearts out, with no luck. The more successful singers have

Bat detecting
at night,
listening in to
high-frequency
sounds in the
woods in
Tunbridge Wells,
Kent.

bigger bodies, and therefore deeper voices; they are the Barry Whites of the *Mystacina* world.[67] The only other bat species known to use a lekking system is Africa's hammer-headed fruit bat: bulbous-nosed males generate spectacular hoots with their huge larynxes to attract passing females.[68] In contrast to such macho displays, the male *Myotis grisescens* or 'gray bat' of the southeastern United States has been known to occasionally forego sex for babysitting.[69]

A few years ago, bats made the headlines for being one of the only species apart from humans to perform oral sex. Researchers in China had observed female fruit bats licking their partners' penises during the act of coupling in order to prolong the act, whether for pleasure or in order to increase the chances of pregnancy, we can only guess. The paper 'Fellatio by Fruit Bats Prolongs Copulation Time' caused much hilarity in the media, and even sparked a sexual harassment scandal in an Irish university when a male academic suggested to a female colleague that they discuss the paper's findings.[70] More recently, Indian researchers have noted that it's not just boy bats that have all the fun, publishing a paper titled 'Cunnilingus Apparently Increases Duration of Copulation in the Indian Flying Fox, *Pteropus giganteus*'.[71]

Mating and reproducing might be a saucy affair in warmer climates, but for temperate bats, hibernation poses serious problems, as during winter pregnancies cannot grow, and nor can sperm be produced. For this reason, reproductive cycles are split over two seasons. What is known as 'spermatogenesis' takes place in spring and summer, and mating follows in autumn (it may even continue during hibernation, when there's not much else to do). Although no new sperm is being produced during this time, there is enough stored sperm to mean that male bats can keep at it, even in winter. The foetus will not grow in the hibernating female, however, so some bat species have developed sperm storage in the female; fertilization takes place as soon as ovulation occurs in the spring. Other bat species have it figured out differently – fertilization occurs after mating in autumn and the fertilized egg develops into what is known as a blastocyst, a pre-embryonic structure, held in the uterus through hibernation, which can start growing again in the spring.[72] In some species, if energy needs

An adult male Chapin's free-tailed bat, *Chaerephon chapini*, in Zimbabwe. The crest remains hidden except during courtship, when it spreads like a peacock's tail.

cannot be met during pregnancy, a mother may actually reabsorb her embryo.[73] But perhaps the strangest of all the stories about bats and reproduction are the reports that, among a certain species of Malaysian fruit bat, males can lactate as well as females. Aside from freak mutations, this happens nowhere else in the mammalian world.

As already noted, bats subsist on a huge variety of food types. Most species are exclusively insectivorous, but others eat fruit, flowers, nectar, pollen, leaves, amphibians, fish, smaller bats and other small mammals. Some are very specific in their diet: for example, the Carolliinae family show a preference for the fruit of the pepper (*Piperaceae*) family, which they eat 'corn-on-the-cob' style. These bats can defecate more than 3,000 seeds a night,[74] a fantastic service to rainforest regeneration, particularly given that seeds that have passed through a bat's digestive tract are far more likely to germinate. Others bats are more catholic in their taste: Allen noted of a leaf-nosed bat he kept in captivity over a six-month period that it ate 25 house mice, thirteen bats and three birds, 'as well as a considerable ration of banana'.[75] According to Allen, South America is a hotbed of banana-crazy Chiroptera: ripening bananas are attacked by 'hordes of hungry bats' who will even squeeze through crevices in mud huts to get at the fruit.[76]

Of all 1,331 species of bats, however, it is the three who dine solely on the blood of other animals that people find most fascinating. They are *Desmodus*, *Diphylla* and *Diaemus*: the vampires. Especially sensitive to breathing noises, vampire bats also have heat sensors in their noses for locating capillary-rich areas of skin, and enlarged, sharp-edged canines and incisors that lack enamel, to enable self-sharpening.[77] These are the bats' precision tools for clipping the fur of their intended victims and painlessly opening a shallow wound. Anticoagulant in the bats' saliva prevents the blood clotting and a grooved tongue helps

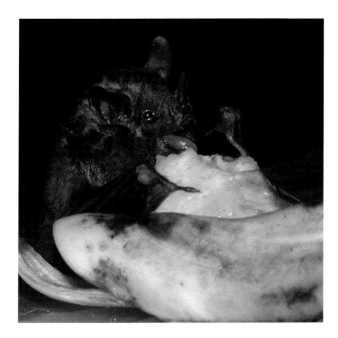

Carollia perspicillata, Seba's short-tailed bat, happily feeding on a banana.

to convey blood rapidly into the mouth.[78] This anticoagulant has been named Draculin and is being studied in relation to human blood thinning for stroke and heart attack victims. Success in this field might go some way to ameliorating the routinely bad press these bats attract.

Vampire bats are frequently portrayed as nature's villains, although unlike carnivores, they rarely kill the animals whose blood they steal. It is important to remember that vampire bats are small – only around 9 cm long – and they take just a table-spoon of blood per night, not enough to seriously harm cattle.[79] They behave like little more than outsize mosquitoes, yet hyper-bolic language is routinely employed when describing vampire bats. They are accused of possessing 'uncanny watchfulness' and

A bat sucking blood from a guinea pig, from Jean Painlevé's film *Le Vampire* (1945).

of 'deliberately' stalking their 'victims'; they 'gouge' and 'attack'; they 'gorge' and 'feast'.[80]

There is no doubting the sinister air of the vampire bat caught by the French scientist and film-maker Jean Painlevé's sensitive if somewhat surreal camera. Painlevé's nine-minute *Le Vampire* (1945) intercuts sequences from F. W. Murnau's 1922 classic *Nosferatu* with footage of a vampire bat bestowing its 'deadly kiss' upon an awake but impassive guinea pig, 'which it slyly approaches like a coquettish Quasimoto'.[81] The film is excruciating as viewers hope the gormless guinea pig will shake off the pint-sized bully, but the vampire feasts on the passive vegetarian, to the unlikely strains of Duke Ellington. Apparently Painlevé saw affinities between the parasitic bat and the 'brown pest' of Nazism which had overrun his native France at the time of filming, comparing the way the postprandial bat extended its wing before going to sleep to a Nazi salute.[82] Critic Ralph Rugoff wrote that Painlevé delighted in presenting his subjects as 'uncanny hybrids that, for all their foreignness, call to mind things close to home'.[83] Here, Painlevé suspends his usual empathetic sensibility towards traditionally unlovely creatures in order to make a metaphoric statement about the plight of France. Rugoff notes that Painlevé's films operate on an 'alternating rhythm of seduction and repulsion' and the same might be said of the human response to bats in general, not just the notorious vampires.[84]

The details of vampire bats' feeding habits make them difficult to champion: they drink up to 60 per cent of their own body-weight in a meal, and often begin to urinate while they are still feeding, since, with all that extra baggage, a return flight to the roost would be an impossible feat. *Desmodus* achieves flight via the ability to perform a kind of 'super push-up' – creepily, this bat can jump from the ground to a height of 90 cm.[85] An engorged belly during feeding is doubtless the origin of this bat's full name: *Desmodus rotundus*. Unsurprisingly, but disappointingly, this is a detail of vampiric physiology that has been overlooked in vampire fiction; imagine a Dracula who began peeing in the midst of a bloodsucking frenzy, or a *Twilight* in which the vampires were tubby overeaters who frequently soaked their designer jeans. Instead, the vampires in the *Twilight* saga are heroin-chic thin, and have skin that glitters like diamonds in the sunlight. Vampire bats might not have shiny skin, but many insectivorous bats have an almost equally glamorous attribute: sparkly poo, owing to the high percentage of shiny wings and carapaces that they chew and excrete.[86]

Whether sparkly or not, and fertilizing properties aside, going into a bat cave can be 'like going into an ice factory in which an ammonia pipe has burst'.[87] Bats can survive in an atmosphere that would be lethal to humans by lowering their metabolic rates. Carbon dioxide accumulates in the bats' blood and in respiratory mucus, and this neutralizes the ammonia and protects the lungs.[88] It may not be a glamorous superpower, but it is another extraordinary adaptation. Wherever bats thrive, their diversity continues to amaze. But more often than not, as we shall see in the next chapter, the dazzling differences between bats and us make them unfairly reviled and unnecessarily feared.

2 Bats in the Belfry: Myths, Madness and Melancholia

Historically, and in almost all corners of the globe, bats have inspired fear and revulsion. Long before tales of blood-sucking bats were relayed from the tropical Americas back to Europe, bats were already disliked and feared, and at the least considered to be pests or vermin, if not veritable agents of evil. Any association with bats in European art and literature could only signify madness, melancholia or, worse, sympathy for the Devil. In artistic depictions, sporting bats' wings was a sure signifier of satanic affiliation, while in real life, bats seen hovering in your vicinity might be evidence enough for your execution. Such was the enmity towards bats and their intimate association with evil that in 1332, Lady Jacaume of Bayonne in France was publicly burned to death because 'crowds of bats' were seen about her house and garden.[1]

What are the roots of the religious opprobrium reserved for bats? In the biblical book of Baruch, considered canonical by Catholics and some Christian Orthodox branches, smoky idols in darkened temples are described as being covered in bats, birds and cats, and 'By this ye may know that they are no gods' (6:23). In Leviticus, alimentary injunctions include bats in the list of unclean birds: 'among the fowls . . . they shall not be eaten, they are an abomination: the eagle, and the ossifrage, and the osprey . . . the stork, the heron . . . and the bat' (11:13–19). The very next line, 'All fowl that creep, going upon all four', may be a reference to bats, which can creep on the ground or across the ceilings of caves; while in Isaiah (2:20) idols of silver and gold are cast to bats and moles as symbols of the lowly, dark and unenlightened.[2]

In striking contrast to the opprobrium reserved for the bat in the Judaeo-Christian tradition, an Islamic story portrays the bat as pious. It is none other than Jesus (Isa) who, with Allah's permission, fashions a bat from clay. He does so because he is fasting for Ramadan, but mountains obscure the setting sun, so Jesus is unsure when it is proper to begin eating. The bat, which emerges from its cave each sunset, becomes an alarm clock for the faithful.[3] Yet across various cultures, including those of the Middle East, angels and demi-gods are most often portrayed as human figures sporting the wings of a bird. This is deemed a noble mutation, while a human depicted with bat wings is repugnant. As mammals it would make more sense for humans to sprout membranous wings than feathered ones, yet leathery appendages across various art histories usually indicate a character's evil essence. Such sinful hybridity represents an inversion of the established order, of which bats, with their propensity for hanging upside down, are the perfect symbols.

The satanic attributes we take for granted today, such as horns, hoofs, a tail, red colouring, bat wings and an indispensible goatee, are relatively recent concoctions. Medieval depictions of Satan and his demons were once as unregulated as spelling. The Prince of Darkness could be a large furry beast with huge animal ears, perhaps horns and clawed (rather than hoofed) feet, with serpents issuing from selected orifices, or could have a human face in place of his genitalia, but only occasionally did he and his hordes have bat wings. Like the miniatures of Hindu, Islamic and Buddhist schools, medieval European demons were most often represented as wingless beasts with horns, googly eyes and tusk-filled mouths set to devour hapless humans.

The Fall of the Rebel Angels, painted in 1345 by an anonymous master of the Sienese School, provides an early European example of the now archetypal bat-winged devils. In this panel a clear distinction is made between the feathered wings of the good angels and the pointy, leather-clad wings of those they are casting from heaven. The pitch-black silhouettes of Satan and his followers leap out against the gold firmament of heaven. It is as though the very instant the angels turned from God their feathers fell out, or were burned to cinders, leaving behind only the naked black leather of bats' wings. They plunge to their eternal damnation, most of them head downwards, just as bats hang. By depicting them as upside down, inverted and in negative, this painting implies that the bat is the ultimate anti-angel.[4]

John Baptist Medina, the first illustrator of John Milton's *Paradise Lost* (1667), oscillated between depicting Satan with

Whether idolatrous or pious, bats do seem to enjoy frequenting sacred sites. Here *Taphozous nudiventris*, or naked-rumped tomb bats, make their home in the Modhera Sun Temple, Gujarat, India.

Master of the Rebel
Angels, *The Fall of
the Rebel Angels*,
c. 1340–45, oil
painting.

feathery and leathery wings. And while Milton himself often refers to Satan's 'winged' status, calling him 'the flying Fiend' (2:643), he never explicitly states that Satan bears the wings of a bat. By the nineteenth century, however, the French illustrator Gustave Doré capitalized on centuries of anti-bat iconography to portray Milton's Satan as the ultimate Romantic anti-hero, with a pair of dramatically pointy bat wings. The European equation of bats with the progenitor of all evil followed European explorers around the globe, impacting the way they viewed exotic fauna. When James Cook made his first voyage to Australia in 1770, one of his sailors, coming upon a flying fox for the first time, was terror-stricken, and ran back to his landing party declaring he had met a real live devil![5]

Bats in European art weren't always necessarily evidence of the Devil himself, but were certainly associated with the negative and darker forces of life, such as torments of the body and soul. Albrecht Dürer's famous engraving *Melencolia I* (1514) features a bat-like creature hovering in the top left corner, emblazoned with the eponymous affliction, from which artists in particular were thought to suffer. Dürer's bat not only announces the subject of the print but may propose a cure, as boiled bats were prescribed in antiquity to treat the accumulation of melancholic black bile in the spleen.[6]

In 1625 Francis Bacon wrote in his *Essays and Councils* that 'Suspicions amongst thoughts are like bats amongst birds, they ever fly by twilight,' and by that batty association immediately announced that these were thoughts that must be repressed or at least well guarded.[7] Over a century later the same murky, mistrustful association of bats with impure thoughts is illustrated by Francisco Goya's etching *The Sleep of Reason Produces Monsters* (c. 1799). This gloomy print depicts the artist asleep, with owls and shadowy bats looming above him. Goya's *Sleep* echoes Dürer's

Melencolia as it too can be read as a portrait of the artist, as well as an allegory of the troubled life of the artist in general. While the owls are well lit, the bats are in full silhouette, growing larger as they ascend, while the topmost bat appears to be wheeling around, perhaps preparing to attack the ill-fated sleeper. If these shadowy bats and birds are figments of the artist's imagination, he is clearly not in control of his creations; they may possibly even turn on their maker, while simultaneously goading him to produce ever more hideous material (one of the owls proffers a pen in its claw). Goya may have been alluding to the terrible power he wielded as an artist in bringing to life the darker side of humanity. The title remains tantalizingly ambiguous: is it a hiatus in reason's vigilance that produces monsters? Or is reason itself a kind of 'sleep' that is ultimately disastrous?

Bats make another unforgettably macabre appearance in Goya's oeuvre: his *Disasters of War* series of etchings (created between 1810 and 1820 but not published until 1863) includes a terrifying scene titled '*Las resultas*' or 'The Consequences', in which the ravages of war are figured as a group of bats wheeling around, and feeding upon, a human corpse. In particular, one giant bat with an almost human face perches upon the corpse's chest and, with a mouth more akin to a hoover than that of a vampire bat, sucks the very life out of the cadaver.

For William Blake, a mind that exudes a bat-like form is necessarily sacrilegious. In 'Auguries of Innocence' (*c.* 1803) he waxes poetical about God's creatures and affirms a sympathetic relationship between humans and animals, yet 'The bat that flits at close of eve / Has left the brain that won't believe.'[8] This is widely interpreted as meaning that the bat embodies the damned soul of the infidel,[9] a hangover from medieval Christian imagery and not at all in keeping with Blake's sensitivity towards robins, pigeons, hares, horses and even flies. In dressing heresy in bat's

'Me miserable! which way shall I fly / Infinite wrath, and infinite despair?': one of Gustave Doré's illustrations for John Milton's *Paradise Lost* (1866 edn).

In Albrecht
Dürer's famous
1514 engraving
Melencolia I, a bat
holds the title and
possibly the cure
for the eponymous
affliction.

Francisco Goya,
*The Sleep of Reason
Produces Monsters*,
No. 43 from
Los caprichos
(The Caprices),
c. 1799, etching
with aquatint
and other
intaglio media.

wings, Blake continues a lineage which stretches its membranous expanse from *The Fall of the Rebel Angels* to George Méliès' *Le Manoir du diable*. Made in 1896, the year before Bram Stoker published *Dracula*, Méliès' silent short film features two instances of a flapping bat transforming into the Devil. While Stoker utilized the same transformation in his terrifying account of an aristocratic vampire's insatiable appetites, Dracula is not, like Satan, the lord of *all* evil, but a specific example of darker forces, one

who has taken the Devil's calumnious association with bats under his own wing.

Stoker's *Dracula* crystallized an inchoate set of associations between evil bats, vampire legends and the stranger-than-fiction zoology of the new world. Europeans encountering blood-feeding bats in the tropical Americas were reminded of folktales of vampires from home, creating an indelible connection between bats and blood-suckers that lingers to this day. Before tales of bats that lapped blood filtered back to Europe, vampires in the 'old countries' bore little relation to Chiroptera. The humanoid fanged fiends did have a propensity for shapeshifting, but were more likely to assume the forms of cats, dogs, sheep, wolves, snakes, birds and horses than the bats we now associate with vampiric metamorphosis.[10] The common European term 'vampire bat', applied to the three species of blood-feeders found in the tropical Americas, is typical of the colonial interpretation of the New World through the lens of the Old, akin to naming a South American vine 'passion flower' because of the alleged Christian symbolism to be found in its showy blooms.

In 1565 Girolamo Benzoni wrote from what is today Costa Rica of bats 'pecking' his hands and feet as he slept,[11] although it is doubtful that this had any part to play in the European vampire hysteria which reached its peak in the 1730s, during which time people accused posthumously of crimes were dug up and had stakes smashed through what was left of their hearts.[12] Voltaire wrote in his *Philosophical Dictionary* that 'Nothing was spoken of but vampires, from 1730 to 1735,'[13] and not long after this the Comte de Buffon used the word 'vampire' in relation to South American bats in his 1749 *Histoire naturelle*.

Vampire bats, however, were not formally described in scientific literature until 1810, when the French naturalist Geoffroy Saint-Hilaire referred to a *Phyllostoma rotundum* found in Paraguay, describing its characteristic underbite and expressing surprise that Buffon had exaggerated its size.[14] The vampire went through several name changes: in 1832 while in Chile, Charles Darwin witnessed what was then referred to as *Desmodus d'orbignyi* in *The Zoology of the Voyage of the HMS Beagle*. Darwin's sighting of the troublesome vampire attached to a horse's withers was fortuitous since, he wrote, 'The whole circumstance has lately been doubted in England.'[15] Stories of giant blood-sucking bats were becoming too fantastical, and, following Saint-Hilaire, Darwin literally cut them down to size, recording that the bat was little more than 7 cm or 3 inches long, and that the horse was fine after a day's reprieve from being saddled.

In spite of Darwin's even-handed perspective, at the close of the nineteenth century, Stoker chose to capitalize on the sensationalist potential of blood-sucking bats. His classic tale of an undead Eastern European count who sails to London to feast on fresh blood and the band of vampire killers who try to stop him hardly requires summary here, so imprinted are the key sequences in the Western popular imagination, including those featuring bats. Suffice it to say that Stoker ignored scientific data such as the vampire bats' diminutive stature, and the fact that they cannot drain a human or animal of blood any more than a mosquito can.[16] Instead, he has the virile American Quincey Morris regale his fellow vampire killers with a tale from 'the Pampas' (a region just south of the vampire bat's true range). Morris's favourite mare was attacked by 'one of those big [sic] bats that they call vampires', until 'there wasn't enough blood in her to let her stand up, and I had to put a bullet through her as she lay.'[17] Even Professor Van Helsing proves a poor naturalist when he talks of 'some islands of the Western seas' where bats hang like giant pods in trees and attack sleeping sailors, who by the morning are found to be 'dead men'.[18] Later in the tale, a London physician tending a bitten child

opines that this might be the handiwork of a bat. He acknowledges that the vast majority of bats are harmless, but that 'there may be *some wild specimen from the South of a more malignant species*'.[19]

Certainly, bats get bad press in *Dracula*, in second-hand stories or observed at first hand flapping their 'silent and ghostly way' or else 'angrily against the window panes'.[20] The implication is that they are either Dracula's messengers or the shapeshifting Count himself. Yet they are by no means his exclusive animal characteristic: dogs and wolves howl when he is near, and horses rear. Dracula is compared to another blood-feeder, the leech, as well as to a lizard, because he crawls from a window '*face down*'.[21] Surprisingly, Stoker misses this opportunity to use a bat simile, since bats are well known for inversion and for scaling vertical surfaces, a facility which puts them in the unclean company of other 'vermin' such as frogs and flies, and nauseates Jonathan Harker as he recounts this 'unnatural' scene in his diary.

In fact, *Dracula* has more to do with wolves than bats; lupine menace permeates the novel. No doubt this has been played down in contemporary vampire narratives to fit with the currently fashionable 'werewolves versus vampires' dichotomy, in, for example, the *Underworld* series and *The Twilight Saga*.[22] An earlier filmic incarnation of *Dracula*, F. W. Murnau's *Nosferatu* (1922), was the tale of an albino, pointy-eared freak, and there were no bats in this chilling silent movie, but plenty of rats. Later, the Count was sexed up as a darkly handsome aristocrat played by Bela Lugosi in 1931, a portrayal which became the standard depiction of Dracula, in essence as a stylized human bat. Lugosi wears a black cape, itself not unusual for a European count, but this one features a pointed collar which echoes the spiky tips of a bat's wings, as does the Count's widow's peak, his sharply contoured eyebrows, his darkened lips. His tortured, grasping hands and slow creep towards his victim both mimic the stealthy vampire bat.

Bela Lugosi as Dracula, from the 1931 movie of the same name.

Within the film, Dracula is synonymous with a large bat whose flapping form precedes his powerful entrance. Yet Lugosi is a gentleman; he grimaces but never bares his fangs on camera – that is left to the imagination. The British Hammer Horror films, however, were unapologetically fang-tastic. They debuted their version of *Dracula* starring Christopher Lee in 1958 and made sequels well into the 1970s, by which time they had truly bled the series dry.

In order to maintain its shock value in a changing social landscape, the implied predatory sexuality of *Dracula* was amplified with each successive filmic remake, reaching a crescendo with Francis Ford Coppola's inventive, sensuous, but ultimately flawed adaptation of 1992. Coppola's take is hallucinatory and ravishing, like a painting by the Symbolist Gustave Moreau. Red as the signifier for blood is everywhere, in robes, dresses and tapestries, and at times blood itself fills the screen; its molecules appear to copulate in a frenzy of contagion. Sex is not just implied, it is viscerally enacted: Dracula, played with unmatched perversity by Gary Oldman, appears in bestial form and penetrates Lucy Westenra while she writhes in a sexualized trance. This Dracula is the ultimate shapeshifter: his age, attire and species fluctuate dramatically. Later, when surprised during an intimate encounter with Mina Harker, Dracula becomes a batlike demon, a grotesque figure that disintegrates into hundreds of black mice. When he finally dies, this demonic bat is revealed as his true form.

When Gary Oldman isn't looking like a suave Eastern European count, he becomes a bat-like demon, in Francis Ford Coppola's *Bram Stoker's Dracula* (1992).

Mathew Beresford suggests that contemporary audiences are by now so familiar with vampires that they expect something different, a 'twist' to hold their attention.[23] There has been such a burgeoning of the genre that many of the old tropes, including bats, have become redundant. But while the Dracula tale and vampire movies in general have become increasingly heterogeneous, a parallel movement in popular culture has seen the

taming of Count Dracula into something camp and comedic. Lugosi proved that he was exceptionally good at spoofing himself, and in *The Devil Bat* (1940) played a mad doctor dedicated to creating 'killer bats' in a laboratory. Carrying around a specimen bat like a desiccated handbag, he hooks it up to nefarious machinery so that it grows exponentially. The doctor persuades the men he wants to kill to wear an aftershave of his own concoction, which acts as a lure for his 'devil bat' to shred their jugulars. While the bat in flight is a poorly fashioned lump of rubber and fur, close-ups depict a charming flying fox licking its chops, no doubt after ingesting a nice grape. Each new murder begets a front-page spread and as panic-stricken headlines fill the screen (as they were wont to do in films of the era), silhouetted bats criss-cross the newspaper articles in which they are the leading story.

The comedic potential of vampire clichés reached its hammy apogee in the American 1960s 'monster' sitcom *The Munsters* with the character Grandpa, who dresses like Lugosi's Dracula, but talks more like a New York cabbie. Grandpa has a pet bat named Igor, who hovers above his head as he performs magical experiments in his basement. While Igor doesn't appear to be operated by strings, his wing strokes are wooden, to say the least. Nevertheless, he is a talented pet: he can fly down to the store for the evening newspaper. Herman Munster, however, the Frankenstein-like head of the house, insults Igor by calling him a 'fly by night' and Igor flaps off in a huff. Herman's wife Lily says that Igor is always throwing tantrums and that he's just a 'spoiled bat'.[24]

In spite or perhaps because of his fearsome reputation, Count Dracula has proved popular as a spoof character for children. The American educational children's television programme *Sesame Street* introduced the puppet character Count von Count in 1972 – caped, fanged and surrounded by a coterie of quivering bats, but whose only vice is that he really loves . . . *to count*. Hardly evil, but more than a little crazed, the Count is one of many instances of cultural production in which bats' peripheral presence signals malady on a sliding scale from quirky to insane.

Lewis Carroll created an indelible if bizarrely genteel portrait of madness: a Hatter who presides over an eternal Mad Tea Party consisting of rather skewed social niceties. Reciting his own warped version of the child's lullaby 'Twinkle, twinkle, little star' he sings:

Twinkle, twinkle, little bat!
How I wonder what you're at!
Up above the world you fly,
Like a tea tray in the sky.
Twinkle, twinkle, little bat!
How I wonder what you're at!

A tea tray, while appropriate to the Hatter's endless party, also recalls the emblazoned bat of Dürer's *Melencolia 1*, whose body and wingspan are flattened out as a device, though in this case for bearing a title rather than tea. Though the Hatter's Tea Party takes place in *Alice's Adventures in Wonderland* rather than the subsequent *Through the Looking-glass*, the bat is symbolic of the mirror-image or inversion of 'normality', since it hangs upside down during the day and becomes active at night (indeed, Alice is told at the Hatter's table that they celebrate 'unbirthdays'). Echolocation expert Donald Griffin asks, 'What rational animal would spend most of its life hanging torpid, head downward, in the dark – abandoning this posture only to pursue flying insects through the night?' [25] While the idea of a 'rational animal' might sound absurd, Griffin thinks it is inevitable that bats be linked in the popular imagination with the eccentric and the insane. Diane

Ackerman suggests that it is because bats fly at night, when humans dream, that we imagine bats moving through a kind of 'dreamtime' in which 'reality is warped'.[26] Kenneth Grant, the British heir apparent to Aleister Crowley's Ordo Templi Orientis, writes that the vampire bat is a zootype of the hanged man, which is an inverse of the crucifix, with all the negative freight such an inversion implies. 'It hangs upside down in its "yogic" sleep of satiation, gorged upon the vital fluid of its victims,' and this suggests 'a retroversion of the senses that is a plummeting backwards through the time-space void'.[27]

It is the crepuscular nature of the bat, of things flying between day and night, that gives us a clue to the unease bats awaken in people. Bats demonstrate 'betweenness' in their relation to the diurnal cycle, and physiologically, seemingly falling outside of known categories. This idea is remarkably pan-cultural, and myths the world over tell stories in which the bat cannot decide if it is a mammal or a bird. *Aesop's Fables* include a story called 'The Birds, the Beasts and the Bat'. The birds and beasts were at war with each other, and the bat switched allegiances, claiming kinship with whoever was winning. When peace was finally proclaimed, both groups realized that the bat had played turncoat and banished him to live a nocturnal life, the moral being that 'Those who practice deceit must expect to be shunned.'[28]

Humans have an innate mistrust of hybridity; the monsters of our collective imagination are chimerical conglomerations – dragons, griffins, harpies and so on. When something is neither fish nor fowl, confusion begets fear, explaining the stickability of Linnaeus and his *Systema naturae*, which classifies all living creatures once and for all, delivering us from superstition into the orderly world of vitrines, formaldehyde, pins and labels. The Comte de Buffon wrote in his encyclopaedic *Natural History* that the bat is 'half a quadruped and half a bird', and therefore 'a monstrous being', an 'imperfect quadruped, and a still more imperfect bird'.[29] The idea of bats being poorly fashioned is an old one: a Germanic folk tale explains the bat as Satan's shoddy facsimile of God's perfect swallow, accidentally including 'ears like a cat, a tail like a rat, and leather wings'.[30] The nineteenth-century critic John Ruskin declared: 'A swallow is a perfect creature of a true gens; and a field-mouse is a perfect creature of a true gens; and between the two you have an accurate mongrel – the bat.' He speculates that many may have entertained the fancy of being a swallow, and he himself has humbly envied a field-mouse, but, he asks, 'did ever anybody wish to be a bat?'[31] Writing long before *Batman* comics came on the scene or the philosopher Thomas Nagel wrote an essay asking the question 'What is it like to be a bat?', it is clear that Ruskin expected the answer to his rhetorical question would be a resounding 'no.'

Poetic fastidiousness about bats continued into the twentieth century, exemplified by D. H. Lawrence's manifest disdain in the poems he writes about batty encounters in Florence in the early 1920s. In 'Man and Bat', Lawrence enters his bedroom to discover what he assumes is a bird, 'Flying round the room in insane circles'.[32] The indication of madness cues the reader that it is not a bird at all, but a 'disgusting' bat:

With a twitchy, nervous, intolerable flight,
And a neurasthenic lunge,
And an impure frenzy . . . [33]

What follows is a gut-wrenching scene as the poet tries desperately to expel the frightened animal as it continues flapping in circles. Lawrence is every bit as frenzied as the bat, waving at it with his handkerchief, to no avail. Eventually the bat is so tired that it stops flying and Lawrence is forced to examine its 'bead-berry eyes' and 'nut-brown, fine fur'. But the poet feels no compassion for the creature: its velvety coat doesn't seduce him, and 'it might as well have been hair on a spider'.[34] As far as Lawrence is concerned, the bat is 'something unclean' and he is vehement that it 'must not squat, nor hang, obscene, in my room!' He lunges and the bat starts to fly again, 'a clot with wings, / Impure even in weariness'.[35] By this time, the reader is as exhausted as both bat and poet (it is a six-page poem). Finally, the bat falls; Lawrence picks it up in a flannel jacket and throws it out of the window. Later, the poet imagines he sees it among its brethren flying at dusk, 'Dipping with petty triumphant flight', and revelling in its escape.[36]

In another poem titled simply 'Bat', Lawrence is watching the sunset over the Arno river, and is puzzled that swallows are flying so late. He notices their serrated wings and then realizes in horror that the swallows have 'changed guard' with the bats, and this leads to an 'uneasy creeping' in his scalp.[37] Unkindly, he calls the bats 'little lumps' and 'wildly vindictive' (the latter seems a better description of his own predisposition to the poor pipistrelles). He ends:

Hanging upside down like rows of disgusting old rags
And grinning in their sleep.
Bats!

In China the bat is symbol for happiness.

Not for me![38]

Fifty years later another literary anti-hero gets in an ineffectual flap about bats, although these leather-winged creatures happen to be a figment of his drug-addled imagination. Hunter S. Thompson begins his semi-autobiographical hallucinatory epic *Fear and*

THE BATS OF VENICE

I PIPISTRELLI DI VENEZIA

Dr. Edoardo Vernier and Jeremy Deller

British artist Jeremy Deller doesn't share D. H. Lawrence's fastidious attitude towards Italian bats, but distributed this free leaflet at the 2003 Venice Biennale.

Loathing in Las Vegas (1971) with a sequence in which the two central characters Raoul Duke and Dr Gonzo are on a cocktail of drugs and speeding through the California desert freeway in a convertible.

> And suddenly there was a terrible roar all around us and the sky was full of what looked like huge bats, all swooping and screeching and diving around the car, which was going about a hundred miles an hour with the top down to Las Vegas. And a voice was screaming: 'Holy Jesus! What are these goddamn animals?'[39]

While in Goya's era it was the sleep of reason that produced monsters, for Thompson it is *lack* of sleep, sustained by amphetamine abuse and countless other stimulants, that impels dark, wheeling shapes to stream from the depths of the psyche.

Some time later, when Dr Gonzo veers off the road and screeches to a halt, Duke's paranoid psychosis takes over, and he yells, 'We can't stop here. This is bat country!'[40] In the 1998 movie version directed by Terry Gilliam, Johnny Depp plays Duke, who thrusts and parries a flacid fly-swatter to keep the imaginary creatures at bay, while clouds of animated bats fly across his sunglasses, swarming like motes in his permanently agog eyeballs. It's worth noting here that a 'cloud' of bats is the official collective noun, rather poetic, but also somewhat murky, as if suggesting compromised acuity.[41] It is far better, however, than 'a murder of crows' or 'an unkindness of ravens'.[42] All things considered, bats got off lightly this time.

Bats' association with mental malady and their frequent depiction in proximity to the human cranium might be related to the irrational and oft-quoted fear that bats get tangled in human hair. There is little or no evidence of this actually occurring, since bats are excellent navigators and sensibly afraid of people. Australian bat researcher Tim Pearson laments the lack of veracity in this old wives' tale – otherwise he would ask long-haired volunteers to stand outside at night, and pull bats from their hair.[43] Unsurprisingly, setting up bat traps is a far more complicated affair.

Screen print by Joe Petro III, Kentucky, based on the original artwork *Bats Over Barstow* by Ralph Steadman, originally printed in Hunter S. Thompson's *Fear and Loathing in Las Vegas* (1974).

It isn't just the thought of having a creepy critter tangled in their tresses that makes some people's skin crawl – in French folklore such an encounter portended a doomed love affair, while in Ireland a bat escaping with a human hair would result in that person's eternal damnation.[44] Less dramatically, folk beliefs from various locations warn that a bat alighting in your hair will lead to your crowning glory grizzling, greying and eventually falling out (though it is a little unfair to blame bats for normal ageing).

Bats celebrated in architecture in Turin, Italy.

Perhaps it is bats' association with rabies that puts them in a precarious position vis-à-vis sanity? Or perhaps it is their seemingly erratic flight that makes them perfect exemplars of the irrational? Eccentric people are called 'batty', which bat lover Russell Peterson charmingly defined as 'having something fluttering within the cranium besides the accepted grey matter'.[45] Similarly, a person may be accused of having 'bats in their belfry', since bats do seem to have a penchant for roosting in bell towers, and, in a bodily architectural schema, the belfry would stand in for the cranium. Bats have a habit of making themselves at home in places of worship, perhaps for no other reason than high, arched ceilings making a passable substitute for cave environments. These are locations where no real demon would dwell, although bat-winged gargoyles have long been the favoured decorations of Gothic church exteriors. The list of batty insults continues: 'ding-bat' is an idiot, perhaps a bat who has been hit in the head by a dinging bell in the belfry? (Given their excellent navigational skills, that would have to be an idiotic bat.) An 'old bat' is an unlikeable old woman, possibly one who is also 'batshit crazy', a more recent phrase which may be related to increasing fears about bats spreading rabies and other diseases via biting or faecal contagion.

While bats never reappear in Thompson's narrative, they set the scene for what will be a truly 'batshit crazy' ride. The 1970s saw a renewed interest in the portentous iconography of the bat. The long association of bats with all things satanic made them perfect fodder for rock 'n' roll as it morphed from colourful, flowery psychedelia to the darker imagery of heavy metal. The most famous instance of bats in the musical charts was theatrical singer Meat Loaf's hit song 'Bat out of Hell', which is full of violence, madness and murder. He warns his (presumably female) lover, the only 'pure' thing in his messy world, that he will have to leave in the morning like a 'bat out of hell' (one wonders if the lady will take this phrase as an insult to her company or even her interior decor?). He promises, however, that he'll come crawling back to her the next night, yet doesn't make it, as he has a motor-bike accident and finally his heart escapes his body like a 'bat out of hell'. The song may not make much sense but nevertheless launched the singer into superstardom, while garish imagery of winged creatures in blazing infernos has been his signature on album covers ever since.

Bat-winged gargoyle, Ulm Cathedral, Münster.

Despite the visuals, Meat Loaf was a family entertainer, at best earning the label of hard rock, but not of heavy metal. The legendary Black Sabbath featured a front man who was just as theatrical as Meat Loaf but much more chilling, if not completely psychotic. Ozzy Osbourne's incantatory singing, crazed eyes and stage antics whipped audiences into frenzies. His habit of flinging offal into the crowd backfired on him, however, when in Iowa in 1982 an audience member threw a live but rather stunned bat on stage. Thinking it was a rubber toy, Osbourne made a show of biting its head off, but unfortunately, for singer and bat alike, it was a real, live (at least until that moment) bat. Osbourne recalls,

> my mouth was instantly full of this warm, gloopy liquid, with the worst aftertaste you could ever imagine. I could feel it staining my teeth and running down my chin. Then the head in my mouth twitched. Oh *fuck me,* I thought. I didn't just go and eat a fucking bat, did I?[46]

Rushed to hospital, Osbourne was given rabies injections, although privately he wondered if anyone would have noticed a difference in his behaviour if he *had* contracted the disease.

While Meat Loaf was singing up a storm about bats out of hell, novelist Martin Cruz Smith wrote *Nightwing* (1977), a thriller about killer bats in a Hopi reservation in the American Southwest. The bloody tale begins with the eerily peaceful birth of a baby bat, in which a mother 'cradles' her hairless offspring, sniffing its scent glands so she can distinguish it from all the other infant bats. Smith calls the bats miracles of evolution: with wing membranes more sheer than surgical gloves, they fly as fast as swallows with colour-blind eyes which 'magnified the light of emerging stars so that the canyon glowed for them and, ahead, the desert was brushed with silver'.[47] But these are not the insect-eating free-tails that inhabit the American Southwest in reality. They are a plague of vampire bats that have travelled north, uncharacteristically eschewing their tropical environs for desert, travelling en masse and eviscerating everything in their path. And they are not 'fluttering like insectivorous bats, but rowing easily with long wings, covering the sky, colouring it with red wings the shape of knives' in a portent of the violence to come.[48]

Smith's bats, like the vampires of myth, are preternaturally programmed for feeding above and beyond all other drives. 'From every other warm-blooded animal they could feel the pulsing of the Food . . . As a result, to the bats there were no natural enemies, not even man. There could be no enemies, when all was the Food.'[49] When the bats attack a camp of Christians, they sound like 'a scattering of dry leaves, then like a tide rushing' over the bodies of the hapless, no longer happy, campers. A woman screams in a 'coat of bats' while the ground is covered with *running* bats and the Christians are spinning 'like maddened dancers'.[50] The action gets battier and bloodier with every chapter, until finally the novel ends with a crescendo of chiropterocide. Readers may experience, however, an inchoate sense of identification with the swarming villains in *Nightwing*, from the tender description of the baby bat's birth at the beginning to a moment when scientists are watching bats' voice imprints on an oscilloscope. While most bats' voice prints were 'graceful shadows shaped like bells or diamonds', the voices of the vampires were 'ragged, almost human'.[51] It is the bats' *human* characteristics – their bloodthirstiness and greed – that make them so terrifying, and yet strangely, compellingly, familiar.

Bat conservation groups are deeply concerned with what has wittily been termed 'Batsploitation' in novels and films – in which bats are no longer mere background scenery in vampiric tales, but are instead the prime protagonists of unlikely gorefests. In a popular culture landscape where the role of the undead has been annexed by zombies while vampires have the taint of the old-fashioned, the new (old) enemy is nature itself, the animal kingdom and the horrors that can be wrought by scientific interference. The rather unimaginatively titled *Bats* (1999), like *Arachnophobia* (1990) or *Snakes on a Plane* (2006), was a B movie designed to exploit species phobia. *Bats* is set in Gallup, New Mexico, where they just happen to be playing *Nosferatu* at the local cinema. When the town is suddenly overrun with carnivorous bats, the shocked sheriff, played by Lou Diamond Phillips, yells 'Christ in a sidecar!' (an unimportant detail which nevertheless gives some sense of the tenor of the tale). The chiropteran villains in *Bats* can slice through windscreens; they have been genetically altered and the culprit, yet again, is a mad scientist. When asked why on earth he would breed monstrous bats, he replies 'That's what scientists do.' In fact, it turns out that the u.s. Government sponsored the batty experiments for weapons development, not as outrageous a proposition as it sounds, as we shall see later. The 'voice of reason' throughout the film is

The 'Batsploitation' movie *Bats,* directed by Louis Morneau in 1999, upset bat conservationists who felt it exploited negative stereotypes about the animal.

BATS

Mayan cylinder vase, late classic period, Guatemala, 680–750 CE.

zoologist Sheila Casper, who tells everyone that bats are harmless and misunderstood. Unfortunately, by the end of the film her statement is blasted to smithereens, like the bats themselves. Sheila and the sheriff comment mid-blast that when it's all over they'll go 'someplace without bats' and have a 'celebratory tequila'.[52] Perhaps the director is having a little laugh on us, since tequila is made from agave, which is . . . pollinated by bats.

An oft-exploited terror-inducing trope in Batsploitation involves entry into one or several caves. While we refer to our ancestors as 'cavemen' due to the preponderance of prehistoric artefacts found in caves, it is unlikely that the cave was literally the preferred dwelling environment for prehistoric humanity. Rather, caves were sacred sites for mortuary or shamanistic ritual, and as such have always been regarded with a mixture of awe and fear. Even bat researchers with no interest in amplifying the Gothic horror of

their encounters nevertheless recount startling scenes such as Jack Couffer's description of the densely populated caves of southern Texas, where literally millions of bats exiting a cave mouth look like 'a heavy snake crawling from a hole and slithering across the sky'.[53] Couffer paints a grim portrait of a photographer who brings huge floodlights into a guano-covered, insect-seething cave. When the lights are switched on, the bats wake up all at once, and, 'roused from slumber, they must answer nature's call; a million bats above our heads must simultaneously empty a million turgid bladders.'[54] A moment later, 'rain' turns to 'hail' and the bats defecate, en masse, small pellets resembling dark grains of rice. The Brazilian free-tailed bats Couffer describes can tolerate a hundred times the concentration of ammonia that humans can. Ammonia is produced less by the bats than by the beetles their guano attracts.[55] Indeed, the beetles' ammonia can reach such

Diego Rivera, *Human Sacrifice before Tohil*, 1931, watercolour. From a series of illustrations of the traditional Mayan epic *Popol Vuh*.

Bat bowl, Mimbres period of the Mogollon culture, c. 1050–1200. These bowls were often burial items, sometimes placed over the face of the deceased and sometimes with a hole punched in the centre. Schematized geometric bats were a recurring motif.

strong concentrations that it bleaches the bats' fur, so that some taxonomists have been fooled into thinking they were studying more than one species. Dermestid beetles eat not only bat droppings, but dropped bats; young bats, sick bats, old bats, all are skeletonized within minutes.

If tales like these are told by scientists, it is no wonder storytellers like Cruz Smith have been inspired to embroider the truth. And he is by no means the first. A mythological skirmish in a bat cave is recorded in the ancient Mayan text *Popol Vuh*, which details the tribulations of two celestial twins, Hunahpu and Xbalanque, who travel through Xibalba, the underworld. They make their way variously through a Razor House, a Cold House, a Jaguar House and a House of Fire. After these horrors comes a sojourn in a hideous 'house of snatch-bats, monstrous beasts, their snouts like knives, the instruments of death',[56] which the brothers avoid by spending the night squeezed up inside their oddly capacious blowgun. When the house grows quiet, Hunahpu peeks out, only to be decapitated by Kama' Zotz' – a giant Death Bat.[57] Savvy Xbalanque replaces his brother's head with a carved squash while Hunahpu's real head rolls onto a ball court, and this is what the brothers use to play ball with the lords of Xibalba. Xbalanque knocks it out of the court; the head is retrieved and surreptitiously switched with the squash, and the game continues. When eventually the squash wears out and splatters its seeds on the court, the lords of Xibalba realize they have been played for fools. All's well that ends well for the brothers; nevertheless, their sojourn in the House of Bats and decapitation by Kama' Zotz' provided Mayan artisans with many opportunities for gruesome bat imagery. But far from being limited to horror fodder, the bat was also the symbol of the fourth month in Mayan cosmology, and the bat glyph had a syllabic value in the Mayan writing system.[58]

Unlike Europeans, whose demonization of bats is rather unfair given the relative harmlessness of temperate bat species, the Maya and other Meso-American cultures had more reason to fear or at least respect bats. These are the regions where not only vampire bats are found, but the largest bat of the Americas, the spectral bat, a carnivore which snatches sleeping birds and rodents by night, dragging them back to its lair full of bones, feathers and other remains.[59] Elsewhere such fears are unfounded, the product of centuries, if not millennia, of myth and misinformation. So, while bats themselves have been used to symbolize unwholesome thoughts, from Bacon, to Goya, to Blake, it is unwholesome thoughts *about* bats which indicate the real human maladies: paranoia, hallucination and pathological anthropocentrism. If bats in the belfry signify madness, then we humans have, for too long, had batty thoughts about bats in our collective, intercultural belfries. It is time to toll the bells, and, as the ever-Gothic Nick Cave sang with appropriate frenzy in 1981, 'Release the bats'!

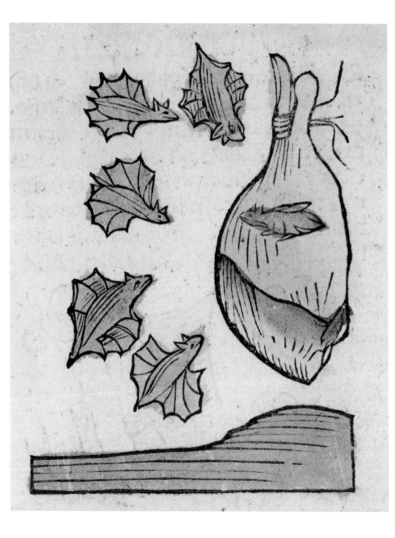

3 Good Luck Charm: Branded by the Bat

While bats are more frequently associated with the murkier side of the human psyche – at best, the mad and the melancholy, at worst, the downright evil – there are nevertheless numerous instances in global art and culture when bats are celebrated. Whether as emissaries of luck in Chinese decorative arts, or as heraldic devices selling goods as diverse as rum, fireworks and superheroes, bats are not always a bad sign. For some, the bat is plainly useful, and its qualities as a pest-controller, pollinator and fertilizer make it a desirable ally. Others find the bat's darker qualities desirable; for example, it is by association with, or absorption of, these qualities that Batman is able to strike fear into the hearts of his enemies, and the trio of witches in *Macbeth* are able to augur the future.

Indeed, bits of bat are the archetypal ingredient for casting spells to do good or evil; Shakespeare's Weird Sisters add 'wool of bat' to the 'hell-broth' in their cauldron (*Macbeth*, IV.i.15), while in *The Tempest*, Caliban curses Prospero by invoking the powers of his dead mother, who was a powerful witch: 'All the charms/ Of Sycorax, toads, beetles, bats, light on you!' (I.ii.339–40). In parts of the Middle East folk cures included bats cooked in various unguents for different ailments: sesame oil for sciatica, jasmine oil for asthma, vinegar to eradicate tumours.[1] Sir Théodore de Mayerne, physician to the royal courts of England and France in

Joseph Meydenbach's *Hortus sanitatis* (The Garden of Health, 1491), wrongfully blamed bats for gnawing at hams hanging in the pantry.

the seventeenth century, devised a notorious 'Balsam of Bats' as a cure for 'hypochondriacal persons'. The ingredients included adders, bats, sucking whelps, earthworms, hog's grease, the marrow of a stag and the thigh bone of an ox.[2] It is unclear whether Mayerne seriously intended his enervated patients to consume this concoction, or whether a miraculous cure would be effected simply by their reading the list of ingredients and vowing never to consult him again.

Mescalero Apache once wore bat-skin bracelets in order to be able to 'stick on a horse' the way a bat clings to cave ceilings.[3] The Hessians of Germany believed that the heart of a bat attached to the arm with a red thread would guarantee the gambler success at cards.[4] Bats' hearts, blood and wings featured prominently in the Hoodoo practices of African Americans in the Southern states of America, and a bat's wing was an essential item for a conjure bag. Nowadays, a toy plastic bat is considered an acceptable substitute.[5]

There is an old English nursery rhyme reportedly sung by little boys: 'Bat, bat, come under my hat,/ And I'll give you a slice of bacon.'[6] Why little boys would want to carry a bat under their hat, except as some kind of good luck talisman, is unclear, but certainly bats were believed to enter houses, just like rats and mice, to steal food, in particular fatty meats. A German word for bat is *Speckmaus* (*Speck* being German for bacon) and an illustration printed in Joseph Meydenbach's 1491 *Hortus sanitatis* (Garden of Health) features bats fluttering around a hanging ham with gluttonous intent. Yet in early nineteenth-century experiments it was found that captive bats offered bacon would rather starve to death than eat it: bats, as is often their lot, had been unfairly scapegoated.[7]

Many folk beliefs featuring bats centre on eyesight, unsurprisingly given bats' uncanny ability to navigate in the dark.

Justin H. Howard, *Aunt Kitty's Stories* (c. 1870).

According to a Chinese herbal, thousand-year-old bats inhabiting certain caves are as white as silver and feed on stalactites; eating such a bat ensures good eyesight and longevity.[8] Other charms featuring bats, however, endow the ability to be *un*seen. Bat researcher Gary F. McCracken recounts a tale of collecting bat blood for genetic testing in Trinidad; a local insisted that if he drank the blood, he would become invisible. Variations on this theme, replacing blood-drinking with carrying a bat's severed eyeball, can be found in places as various as the Tyrol, Brazil and Oklahoma.[9]

Unfortunately, while these charms celebrate bats' magical qualities, the only way to confer these powers on humans involves death and dismemberment for the bat. Nowhere was this more brutally enacted than in the European practice of nailing a live bat head downwards above a doorway as a safeguard against misfortune (though not for the bat!). This sadistic superstition was still extant in the 1920s in parts of England, France and the Netherlands.[10]

The Tempest offers its own counterpoint to the no doubt grisly 'charms of Sycorax' in the persona of Ariel, an ethereal spirit

whose interactions with the natural world are gentle. Rather than dismembering bats in order to cast spells, his magical relationship to these creatures sees him join their world with ease as he sings:

> Where the bee sucks, there suck I.
> In a cowslip's bell I lie;
> There I couch when owls do cry.
> On the bat's back I do fly
> After summer merrily. (v:i:88–92)

Ariel's joyful song conjures a harmonious world of airborne creatures interacting with flora. This is also the world figured in Chinese decorative arts, where bats are frequently depicted as delightfully cheeky harbingers of good luck. Thanks to the word 'bat' being homophonic with the word 'luck', the two have become intimately entwined in millennia of decorative production. In China bats are literally everywhere: on teapots, snuff bottles, belt buckles, embroidery and furniture, often so stylized as to remain unnoticed. Western bat lovers have long thanked the Chinese for providing a bastion of hope in a world of chiroptophobes. Bat biologist Glover Morrill Allen commends China for seeing 'the other side of the shield', while bat advocate Russell Peterson celebrates 'the sensible Chinese' because 'the Oriental mind', being singularly receptive to beauty and form, was able to view the bat in a positive light.[11] However paternalistic these sentiments might sound today, they demonstrate palpable relief that in at least one corner of the globe, bats have been celebrated rather than reviled. Animal author Boria Sax suggests this might be a theological, rather than an aesthetic, issue: among cultures which venerate ancestral spirits, bats are beloved, while those cultures that assume spirits pass on rather than return inevitably perceive bats as demons.[12]

In spite of the Qing Dynasty lasting from 1644 to 1912, it is unlikely that the artisan who fashioned this beautiful object had heard Lewis Carroll's characterization of a bat being 'like a tea tray in the sky'. Yet these mother-of-pearl 'fairy rats' inlaid into lacquer would make a delightful addition to any tea party.

Vintage Japanese matchbox displaying the classic Chinese *wufu* or five bats design.

The *wufu* is China's best-known bat talisman, featuring five of the jaunty creatures facing inwards, often surrounding the character for longevity. *Wufu* means 'five happinesses', namely health, wealth, longevity, virtue and a natural death.[13] Decorative bats are frequently seen in the company of peaches; in China that fruit has lofty connotations with immortality. A bat and two peaches form a rebus meaning 'happiness and longevity, both complete'.[14] Bats in combination with gourds form another symbol of plentiful procreation, but most often they are depicted with clouds, which are also homophonic with good fortune, a doubly auspicious partnership.[15]

Chinese bats are charmingly quirky; highly stylized, their wings often curl into decorative spirals. The bat is often so ornate that it can be mistaken for a butterfly, and the more fanciful Chinese names for bats, such as 'embracing wings', 'heavenly rat', 'fairy rat' and 'night swallow', make them into creatures of fairy-tale rather than of nightmare.[16] Unlike Western depictions of bats flying upwards and out of the frame, Chinese bats are almost always head down, pointing inwards, appropriate to their predilection for hanging upside down.[17] One source suggests that Chinese bats are depicted flying downwards because of their weighty brains, while another points out a pun on the phoneme *dào*, which means both 'upside down' and 'to arrive': hence an upside-down bat makes a popular New Year's decoration because it can be read as 'Luck is arriving.'[18]

The Victoria and Albert Museum is well known for its excellent collection of Chinese decorative arts, where bat motifs make a frequent appearance. This display of Chinese treasures plays a pivotal role in Russell Hoban's 2002 novel *The Bat Tattoo*, in which two partnerless protagonists find each other via the unlikely coincidence that they each sport a bat tattoo based on the same Chinese ceramic bowl. Roswell Clark visits the V&A to see a specific Chinese chair covered with embroidered silk depicting two bats 'dancing in that blue-silk sky like paper kites, their fancy wings all curvy and fringy'.[19] Instead he notices an unassuming white bowl decorated with red bats (which can still be seen in the V&A collection). While anatomically unrealistic, red bats create another rebus symbolizing extensive good luck, red being homophonic with 'vast, abundant'.[20] Roswell is irresistibly drawn to these

Porcelain bowl from Jingdezhen, China, made between 1723 and 1735. This bowl inspired the Russell Hoban novel *The Bat Tattoo* (2002).

particular bats' 'unquenchable high spirits' and chooses his favourite bat to become a tattoo because it's a 'Let's-do-it! Bat'.[21] As he receives the tattoo, Roswell uses metaphors of flight: 'the eighteenth-century bat of the Yongzheng period taxied down the runway into the new century on me.' Roswell wants the airborne mammal to take him aboard, like Ariel on the bat's back, and fly him outside of himself. In this case, bats' flight is not seen as repugnant, as D. H. Lawrence might have it, or awkward, as the Comte de Buffon proclaimed it, but aspirational, a model for rising above the mundane.

The bats which Hoban describes have sharp, serrated wings that are almost translucent, but there are uncountable variations of Chinese bats. There are embroidered bats whose wings become opulent, or ragged and cloud-like; carved wooden bats whose whorled wingtips embellish furniture; and simplified, schematic bats, the kind that are so ubiquitous in blue-and-white Chinese tableware that they almost go unrecognized, looking at first glance more like abstracted birds or pure geometries.

The German poet Rainer Maria Rilke relates bats to pottery by comparing the zigzag of a bat through the air to a crack in a cup. He projects human chiroptophobia back onto the bat – it flies erratically, 'rending through the evening's porcelain', because it is afraid of itself.[22] While in China, the fanciful fairy rat is the apogee of decorative tableware, the Western mistrust of bats is exemplified by Rilke's portrayal of the night-flying creature as disharmonious. Yet in Oriental thought and aesthetics, even 'disharmony' can be rehabilitated as a virtue. In Japan, cracks in pottery are often repaired with gold joinery in a practice called *kintsugi*, transmuting the unlovely and overlooked into treasure. While Western fear and prejudice rends cracks between humans and bats, the Japanese craft of *kintsugi* offers a charming metaphor for repair: gilding makes a feature of that which was once thought ugly, and as we shall see, there are some remarkable examples of gilded, and golden, bats.[23]

The symbolism of bats in Japanese artefacts is more ambiguous than it is in China; nevertheless, bats are treated with a captivating mixture of naturalistic observation and imaginative licence. The Edo period Japanese artist Gosotei Toyokuni II depicted a series of fashionable ladies in woodblock prints, one of whom sports a glorious indigo kimono covered with dark bats (following traditional Chinese imagery, her sash is patterned with gourds). In the top right-hand corner a giant bat hovers, emblazoned with the series' title: *Beauties of the Latest Fashion Compared with the Beauty of Flowers* (c. 1830–35). This use of the bat as a cartouche or titling device within the image recalls Dürer's emblazoned bat in *Melencolia I*, and reinscribes the idea of a *textual* bat. For indeed, don't the outstretched wings of a bat resemble the cover of an open book, its furry stomach the fluttering pages?

While bats in China often represent a busy, utilitarian brand of fertility, their Japanese cousins seem altogether more sensual, as this haiku by the eighteenth-century poet Buson suggests:

Hour of the velvet soft-winged bats . . .
The soft-eyed maid
Throws me a velvet glance.[24]

Such twilight softness seems a world away from Rilke's easily shattered 'evening's porcelain'. Perhaps the subtle, almost imperceptible desire implied by Buson's shadowy creatures is what inspired Evelyn Waugh to describe erotic tension between characters as a 'thin bat's squeak of sexuality' in *Brideshead Revisited*?[25]

In both China and Japan the use of bat imagery in decorative and fine art segued into commercial art, and in the early twentieth century it was common to see cheeky, perky bats adorning

brightly packaged firecrackers and matchboxes, where they became icons of sparkling night-time escapades, and certainly not harbingers of doom or death. Bats come to represent the glamour of the night, what goes on in the shadow world; maybe not drinking blood, but alcoholic spirits, and other more human forms of hedonism, like smoking. Golden Bat, founded in 1906, is Japan's oldest cigarette brand, and still sports a version of the original Art Nouveau packaging: two golden bats facing off on a chartreuse ground. During the Japanese occupation of Manchuria the Kwantung Army followed the shameful example of the British in China and deliberately fostered drug addiction by spiking the tips of Golden Bat cigarettes with small doses of heroin. Profits soared while apathy ruled the masses, but those who perpetrated this cynical abuse of power were later tried as war criminals.[26] Perhaps this shady history added to the brand's notoriety in Japan, rivalling that of Gitanes in France: they were the preferred smoke of numerous Japanese writers. Today, packs of Golden Bat cigarettes can still be found as offerings on gravestones in Japanese cemeteries.

Utagawa Toyokuni II, *Chrysanthemums*, from the *Beauties of the Latest Fashion Compared with the Beauty of Flowers* series, c. 1826.

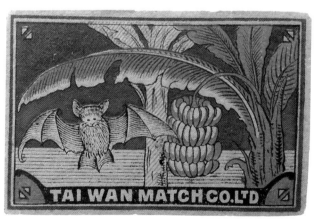

This vintage matchbox features a bat next to a bunch of bananas, a favourite food source for many tropical bats.

Vintage Japanese matchbox, demonstrating the Chinese idea of the connection between bats and good fortune.

In 1931 the writer Ichiro Suzuki and illustrator Takeo Nagamatsu used the famous cigarette brand as a readymade name for a super-hero. The Golden Bat, or Ōgon Bat (pronounced in Japanese *Ohgon Batto*), made his debut in the Japanese *kamishibai*, which translates as 'paper theatre': travelling shows in which professional story-tellers narrate still pictures into a seamless plot. Ōgon Bat was a strange creation featuring a golden skull for a head, a red cape and rapier sword, and may have been inspired by the Phantom of the Opera.[27] Indeed, Ōgon Bat possessed a number of classic superhero characteristics, including a fortress of solitude, super strength, a billowing cape and the ability to fly.[28] Originally from Atlantis, he had been sent forwards 10,000 years in time to battle evil in contemporary Japan.[29] Sequestered in the Japanese Alps, he

Golden Bat Cigarettes, Japan's oldest brand, still sold today.

would come only when sent for by a little girl called Emily. Ōgon Bat fought against bat-like villains as well: Nazo the Emperor of the Universe, with black, bat-like ears, and his own inverse character, Kurayami, the Dark Bat, a character who looked much like himself but with a dark, rather than golden, skull.[30]

Ōgon Bat was the most popular of all the *kamishibai* characters, and following the Second World War made the jump into manga (comics) and anime (cartoons), just as *kamishibai* fell out of favour with the introduction of television. It is telling that one of the last *kamishibai* stories was a rendition of the 1960s American *Batman* TV series.[31] While Ōgon Bat pre-dated the emergence of the original 1939 *Batman* comic by eight years, the *kamishibai* which started with Ōgon Bat bowed out by paying tribute to none

A *kamishibai* artist narrates a story of Ōgon Bat, the Golden Bat, as recently as 2009 in Kyoto.

other than Ōgon Bat's Western counterpart, whom I will discuss further below. In this instance, the bat-as-superhero meme had flown full circle, from East to West and back again. Eventually, Ōgon Bat was made into live action films, such as *Ōgon Batto ga yattekuru* of 1972, translated rather bathetically as *The Golden Bat Shows Up*.

While bats are almost always portrayed as black, there are some species that earn the epithet 'golden', including the Rodrigues fruit bat from Mauritius, which Gerald Durrell described as having fur 'like spun gold'.[32] In Colombia the Tairona made an artform from this paradox – the creature of darkness who shines with golden light – by fashioning elaborate bat-shaped breastplates and pendants out of gold. The Kogi descendants of the Tairona include in their cosmology an 'underground sun of darkness' whose symbol is the bat.[33] In Kogi cosmology bats are considered to be the first animal of creation, born of an incestuous union between this inverted solar deity and his own effeminate son. The Kogi word for bat, *nyuízhi*, may be interpreted as a combination of *nyui* (sun) and *zhi* (worm or penis).[34] Bats have links to fertility and menstruation, since they 'suck blood'. For Kogi women, 'Has the bat bitten you?' is a euphemism for 'Are you menstruating?', while young men judge a girl's nubility by whether or not 'the bat has bitten her'.[35] Tairona breastplates often feature 'bat men' who are part human and part bat and sometimes wear bats hanging from decorative crowns, which themselves symbolize the large ears of certain species of bat.[36]

A less foreboding Latin American manifestation of bat symbolism is the Bacardi Rum logo; with roots in pre-Columbian mythology, it is now thoroughly embedded in the global marketplace. So inseparable is the rum from its insignia that the company's official website features imagery of bats in flight at

Tairona breastplate depicting a bat-man hybrid, Colombia, 900–1600 CE.

sunset, and the sound of bats chittering as you read Bacardi's foundation story. In the 1860s Doña Amalia Bacardí noticed fruit bats in the ceiling of the family distillery (attracted by the smell of molasses) and she insisted on using the bat as Bacardi's logo. Bats were a symbol of good fortune in the family's native Catalonia and also of the local (but sadly no longer extant) Taino Indians,[37] who had seen bats as the souls of the dead, but without fearful connotations. Bat spirits would wait for the sun to go down to come out and 'eat guayaba [guava], have sex, celebrate and dance',[38] behaviours which seem altogether compatible with staying out late and drinking rum.

Bacardi de-emphasizes the lewd vivacity of Taino bat spirits; for the company, bats symbolize 'brotherhood', 'discretion' and 'faithfulness'.[39] The bat logo operates as a good-luck charm which helps the family survive 'whatever fate throws at it'.[40] Much is made of the family's changing fortunes, including earthquakes, fires and prohibition. The distillery has been based in Bermuda since the Cuban revolution, and now the exiled family of rum magnates liken themselves to bats circling: 'one day, when the bat goes home, we will go home too.'[41]

Fortuitously for Bacardi and bats alike, a colony of *Eumops floridanus*, one of the rarest mammals in the world, happens to roost near the Bacardi North America regional office in Coral Gables, Florida.[42] Together with a local bat ecologist, Bacardi ran neighbourhood educational events on the plight of this poor mammal. On a grander scale, Bacardi have sponsored Bat Conservation International video billboards in Times Square, New York, while late family member Luis F. Bacardi founded the Lubee Bat Conservancy, which continues to award annual grants for bat research.

Tequila, however, is the spirit with a real-life bat connection: Mexican long-nosed bats from the genus *Leptonycteris* have co-evolved with night-blooming agave, tequila's vital ingredient.

Agave tequilana, a spiky, blueish plant which grows in the arid northern Mexican desert, is *chiropterophilous*, or bat-pollinated. The fetid-smelling blooms crown a 4.5-m stalk, but herein lies the problem for bats. Since agave is propagated from rootlets, tequila manufacturers don't let the agave mature long enough for it to flower. These harvesting practices harm both bat ecology and plant biodiversity: without cross-pollination, the industry is at risk of monocultural disease.[43] Let's hope that tequila makers can also become bat conservationists (actually, Bacardi owns Cazadores Tequila).

Bats and big business may seem like strange bedfellows, yet bats have been fashioned from the metal most synonymous with wealth, and symbolize prosperity for the Chinese. Others have seen the potential to make a literal buck off the bat's back: in 1925 the Texan physician Dr Charles A. Campbell wrote the treatise *Bats, Mosquitoes and Dollars*. While his primary objective was to point out that insect-eating bats have saved countless humans from malaria simply by snaring their evening meal, his secondary focus was the fact that bat guano was a kind of 'black gold'. He called bats 'sanitary workers' and 'man's best friend' and, determined that bats, like bees, could be 'colonized and cultivated', built monumental bat houses to prove his point.[44] While Campbell's first experiments were failures, he ended up building a house which attracted so many chiropteran residents that it took a full two hours for them to stream out of their living quarters on their nightly hunt for insects. Campbell's roost was in San Antonio, close to Bracken Cave, today known as the largest bat colony in the world. In a contemporary update of Campbell's advocacy, Bat Conservation International promotes Texan bat populations to local councillors as being free organic pest control for farmers. Local farmers might not be *earning* dollars off the bats, but they are certainly *saving* dollars, due to the creatures' nightly forays. In fact, global savings on crop damage thanks to bats have been estimated at many billions of dollars per year.[45]

Guano gathering is still practised at Bracken Cave and all over the world, wherever bats congregate long enough to gift the earth with their potent excrement, feeding all kinds of insects and nurturing cave ecosystems. Guano from insect-eating bats is particularly high in nitrogen, which promotes leafy green growth and is subsequently sought-after fertilizer for lawns, as well as other kinds of 'grass'. Marijuana growers love bat guano and much of it is marketed with zany labels to appeal to gardeners growing more than just petunias.

The 'usefulness' of bats to humans has not always been measured monetarily – strangely, bats have been called upon in

Dr Charles A. Campbell and his municipal bat roost, San Antonio, Texas, 1914. He is standing against one of the supports to give an idea of scale.

Bat guano is still a popular fertilizer.

two major wars, as we shall see. But for one bat researcher who observed roosts in southern Texas during the Second World War, images of money again come into play. Jack Couffer writes that, until witnessing the mass exodus of Brazilian free-tailed bats from Texan caves, he had difficulty conceiving of large sums of money, asking, 'How does one comprehend the *volume* of a million actual dollar bills?' He answers: 'It is a stream of bats, each leathery wing a one dollar bill, carried by a whirlwind, swirling from a vault; a stream twenty feet in diameter, a fast-moving river of worn, fluttering banknotes that flows without slackening for three continuous hours.'[46] According to Couffer, there is an old Texan expression for a well-worn dollar bill, which, 'having achieved the ultimate in limpness through age and careless pocketing', is known as a 'bat-wing'.[47]

So what on earth was Couffer doing, along with a team of assorted oddballs, researching bats in a top-secret programme in the Second World War? Couffer's memoir *Bat Bomb: World War II's Other Secret Weapon* reads like a companion text to *Gravity's Rainbow*, with its bizarre cast of characters and surreal and literally 'explosive' plot. Couffer's story, however, is true: there really did exist a Project X-Ray that intended to strap incendiary devices to individual Microchiroptera. The plan was that thousands of bats would be packaged into bomb-shaped devices, with each plane delivering up to 200,000 of the involuntary kamikaze fighters to the unsuspecting Japanese. Chilled 'bombs' would keep the bats in hibernation; released in daylight, the rudely awakened bats would immediately seek roosting sites in combustible Japanese housing. The incendiary in question, an ancestor of napalm, would be triggered by gnawing on the ignition device as bats struggled to free themselves from their unwanted attachments, thus thousands of fires would erupt simultaneously. Casualties would be low (if you discount the poor incinerated bats) but the ensuing chaos would, it was predicted, bring the Japanese to their knees.

The man behind this madcap scheme, Pennsylvanian dentist Dr Lytle S. Adams, penned an impassioned pitch to President Roosevelt saying: 'As I vision it, the millions of bats that have for ages inhabited our belfries, tunnels and caverns were placed there by God to await this hour to play their part in the scheme of free human existence, and to frustrate any attempt of those who dare desecrate our way of life.'[48] The President endorsed Adams's plan by forwarding his letter to his top brass, with the accompanying note 'This man is *not* a nut.'[49] Project X-Ray got the green light and numerous experiments were undertaken, none of which benefited the bats themselves, although they were temporarily seen as potential saviours rather than pests. In a moment of poetic justice, one of the crucial trials backfired and bats incinerated the entire airstrip, control tower, barracks and fields of the Carlsbad Auxiliary Airfield.[50]

While the Project X-Ray team were setting fire to airstrips with explosive bats, rumours of another secret weapon started to circulate, about a group of scientists trying to make bombs out of atoms. Doc Adams thought it was the 'silliest nonsense'; after all, 'We got a sure thing like the bat bomb going, something that could really win the war, and they're jerking off with tiny little atoms.'[51] However, once the atom bomb became a viable reality, Project X-Ray was cancelled, and the rest is history. Couffer believes that the bat bomb might have been a more 'humane' alternative (for the people of Japan, if not for the bats), with far less alarming conclusions: presumably it wouldn't have led to the same kind of proliferation seen in the Cold War.[52]

The Second World War wasn't the first time the bats of Texas had been called into the service of human battles. Their guano proved to have uses beyond the promotion of plant growth; potassium nitrate, or saltpetre, could be extracted from accumulated droppings, and this was used by the Confederate States during the Civil War to make gunpowder. This may also explain why bats are such popular imagery on Chinese firecrackers, since Chinese first invented gunpowder from saltpetre, likely collected from caves, for showy light displays. The Confederate Army wasn't interested in the visual potentials of gunpowder, however, but its ability to blow apart human bodies. So valuable was this bio-chemical resource during war time that the Texan caves were under regimental guard.[53] Still further back, some Native American tribes saw a relationship between bats and weaponry. The Pomo of California have a story that a bat could chew and swallow a large piece of obsidian and then vomit copious numbers of excellent arrowheads. This tale may have been inspired by the

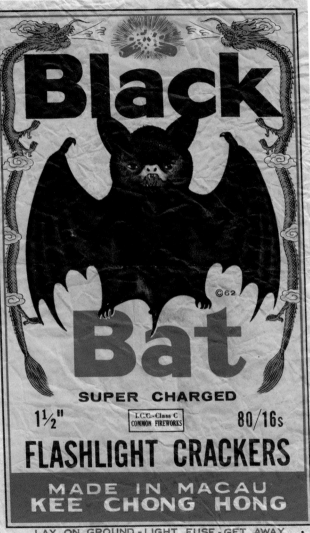

prominent noseleaf of California leaf-nosed bats, whose pointed tip recalls an arrowhead.[54]

Bat-shaped weapons and bat caves are the accoutrements of one of the most enduring cultural icons of the twentieth century, and still alive and well in the twenty-first. Batman seems to be a litmus test for the zeitgeist: his many filmic, cartoon, comic strip and TV incarnations have been by turns heroic, camp, gaudy, ridiculous, dark and brooding. Even the logo itself, like that of Bacardi, has been through countless iterations to keep pace with the tempo of the times.

Batman comics debuted in 1939 during 'prewar jitters' in the United States.[55] Created for DC Comics by writer Bob Kane and illustrator Bill Finger, the nocturnal crime fighter was a bricolage of characters, featuring attributes of Zorro, Sherlock Holmes and Dracula.[56] Although Batman was a hero, he reprised aspects of Stoker's monstrous bloodsucker, lurking with his cape in the shadows. Indeed the very name of his city, Gotham, evokes Gothic architecture and literature. Although its etymology is the rather less glamorous Anglo-Saxon for 'Goat Town',[57] Gotham plays up to its literary associations: the comics' looming, angular portrayal of the city and its dark, seamy underbelly are a twentieth-century update on Gothic fiction while prefiguring the film noir of the 1940s and '50s.[58] In the 1960s Batman made the leap to television and, embodying the goofy, colourful pop-cultural sensibilities of the era, drained the character of any seriousness or believability. While a bat-like propensity to scale walls induces revulsion in *Dracula*, this same capability is parodied to exceptionally camp effect in the *Batman* television series; it is made obvious that Batman and his side-kick Robin are walking normally while the camera has been tilted. The show's extreme self-mockery and facetious humour has been called 'subversive', although leading man Adam West purportedly saw his character

Black Bat firecrackers, Hong Kong.

These United States postage stamps demonstrate the different sides of Batman imagery: grim and macho, or colourfully camp, as well as the character's enduring popularity. These stamps were printed in 2006, almost seventy years after the release of the first Batman comic.

as a modern-day Hamlet.[59] In the 1950s psychiatrist Fredric Wertham had declared the comics' portrayal of Batman's relationship with Robin as 'psychologically homosexual' at a time when sexologists were still using the term 'inversion' for homosexuality, a heteronormatively loaded word which nevertheless seems appropriate when considering the role of the upside-down bat in popular imagination and the bat cave as Batman's closet.[60] Much of the humour of the TV series is derived from the quasi-eroticism of grown-up men in coloured tights and the cheesy lines delivered by Robin in his over-eager desire to be of service to Batman.

The comics rediscovered their darker roots with Frank Miller's 1986 *The Dark Knight Returns*. This brooding, anarchic reprise did away with Robin altogether and inspired Tim Burton's 1989 *Batman* movie, starring Michael Keaton and provoking a flourishing trade in merchandise featuring the Batman logo. Burton and Keaton teamed up again with *Batman Returns* in 1992, in which Keaton sits in a bat cave surrounded by bats, while felines twine themselves around a shiny-vinyl-clad Catwoman, and penguins form the guard of honour at the death of their villainous, fish-breathed namesake. Deleuze and Guattari write that 'every Animal has its Anomalous',[61] and it seems, at least in this film, that Batman and his villains are more anomalous animals than they are extraordinary humans. The Penguin in particular is an abuser of animal armies; fiendishly, he controls swarms of bats to frame Batman and prepares an army of remote-controlled penguins fitted with explosives, not unlike the real life experiments of Project X-Ray's 'bat bomb'.

Joel Schumacher directed the next two films in the franchise, *Batman Forever* (1995) and *Batman and Robin* (1997). Both films open with fetishistic close-ups of the batsuits, including spikes, rubber and even a shot of the armour-plated Bat Butt. Schumacher's

Batman films were more camp, gaudy and downright ridiculous than the TV series, but without its lo-fi charm.

Almost ten years later the *Batman* franchise was rebooted by Christopher Nolan, who returned the hero to his noir roots with grittier, edgier films. In going back to basics Nolan also gets back to bats: in *Batman Begins* (2005) the opening sequence logo is assembled from swarming Chiroptera. This Batman, it seems, has a posse: no prior *Batman* movie has gone into such detail over Bruce Wayne's relationship with his totem animal. Young Bruce falls down the shaft of a disused well, and the disturbed bats roosting there swarm over him. This terrifies the small boy, and when his parents take him to the opera (Boito's *Mefistofele*), performers dressed as demons sporting bat wings renew little Bruce's terror; he begs his father to leave the opera early. This is when a mugger murders the boy's parents, so that bats, fear and anger are forever entangled in Bruce Wayne's psyche. The whole movie is a meditation on understanding and overcoming fear, and is riddled with zen aphorisms which sound as though they have been plucked from the pages of self-help books, but which can all be applied to the human perception of bats: 'You always fear what you don't understand,' 'What you really fear is inside yourself,' 'Men fear most what they cannot see,' 'Embrace your worst fear: become one with the darkness.' Most of these lines are spoken by a martial arts guru played by Liam Neeson, who in another film (or rather, galaxy) mentored the black-caped hero-turned-villain Darth Vader. And it's perhaps not too fanciful to note that in Nolan's *Batman*, our hero's right-hand man in the absence of Robin is Commissioner Gordon, played by Gary Oldman, who also portrayed the most notorious Dracula after Lugosi. This nepotistic game does more than point out that Hollywood is indeed a tight circle; it demonstrates the ubiquity of the recursive figure of the bat-like man, which lurks, omnipresent, in the popular imagination.

The Neeson-trained Wayne returns to the well of his boyhood, site of his ultimate fears, to find that it is connected to a series of underground caves filled with bats. He stands his ground as they swarm around him. He has conquered his fear, but hasn't dispelled it: indeed, when the Scarecrow doses him with a 'weaponized hallucinogen' he sees bats flying out of the mouth hole in the villain's sackcloth mask every time he speaks. Batman acknowledges that bats still frighten him, but now, 'It's time my enemies shared my dread.' He has become one with darkness, catching villains unawares, his seemingly invisible attacks accompanied by the sound of frenzied bat's wings. And Batman has backup – he is able to escape unseen from a building by calling swarms of bats with a sonic device he hides in his shoe. The bats break through glass windows and provide the ultimate mask for our masked hero.

The Dark Knight (2008), Nolan's second *Batman* film, features less bat imagery, unless you consider the mouth of the Joker (played by an extremely sadistic Heath Ledger): leering, scarified and painted, this perma-smile seems to be an eerie echo of the ever-pointier *Batman* logo. The film's technological lynchpin is an invention which collects data from every mobile phone in the city to create a sonic triangulator – essentially echolocation on a mass scale. This feeds into the bat mask and creates glowing eyes with which Batman can 'see' – not only in the dark, but through walls and across vast distances. The film ends with Batman, like his real life bat-kin, taking the blame for wrongs he doesn't commit – he willingly takes on the mantle of scapebat, misunderstood and hunted.

Nolan's third film, *The Dark Knight Rises* (2012), begins in this space of retreat: Batman hasn't been seen on the streets of Gotham for eight years and has passed into legend. An orphan boy compulsively draws bats with chalk on the pavement: a symbol not

In this scene from *Batman Begins* (2005), our titular hero strides out of a building in a chiropteran cloud.

of luck, as the Chinese would have it, but of hope. That this was also the catchphrase of the Obama campaign has had Internet paranoiacs cast Obama as 'the Dark Knight', not least because the two films with that title have release dates coinciding with Obama's terms in office. While Nolan disavowed political readings of the film, *The Dark Knight Rises* undeniably conflates activism with terrorism and has been described as 'audaciously capitalist' and 'radically conservative'.[62] Philosopher Slavoj Žižek outs Batman as a card-carrying member of the elite 1 per cent that the Occupy Wall Street movement named as the problem: 'Arms dealer and speculator – this is the secret beneath the Batman mask.'[63]

This is not the first time *Batman* has inspired political critique. Cultural theorist Andrew Ross noted the ubiquity of the *Batman* logo in 1989 after the release of the Tim Burton film, declaring that the bat totem was 'established in modern Euro-Western cultural iconography as the vampiric defense of white, aristocratic blood'. In *Batman* this image has been 'reinterpreted in the interests of American Gothic, with its celebratory Protestant fantasy of white vigilante justice sweeping the fetid air, masked and invincibly righteous'. For Ross, Batman is inherently racist, and he compares his mask to that of a Klansman.[64] Whether it be the aristocratic Dracula, the millionaire Bruce Wayne or even

Bat-themed outfit for a fancy-dress ball, *La mode illustree,* 1887, by Moret, possibly inspired by *Die Fledermaus.*

Another take on bat-themed evening wear, from the German satirical weekly *Fliegende Blätter,* in 1882.

the wealthy Bacardi dynasty, bats do, it seems, have connections to money and power.

While *Mefistofele* is an appropriately turgid opera to frighten the young Bruce Wayne, there is actually an opera called *The Bat,* or rather, an operetta by Johann Strauss II titled *Die Fledermaus.* This bourgeois comedy of errors premiered in 1874, and centres around a well-mannered revenge plot. The revenge-seeker is Falke who, when dressed as a bat for a costume party, was abandoned, intoxicated, in a public square by a friend. Because of the ridicule he endured, he thus seeks to shame his acquaintance. After an elaborate series of plot twists, Falke finally reveals his

Kama' Zotz', the bat god and emblem of the Mayan city of Copan, Honduras.

hand to his long-suffering friend, declaring, 'That's how the bat gets his revenge!', while the chorus cries: 'O Fledermaus, O Fledermaus, do let your victim go at last.'[65] While *Die Fledermaus* is a far cry from *Batman*, it is nevertheless a story of caped retribution, masks, deception and mistaken identity for which a costumed bat, rather than a cat, rat or fox, was considered most appropriate.

If Gotham City adopted the bat as its logo, its real-world analogue was perhaps Copán, an outpost of the Maya civilization in present-day Honduras. A glyph representing a leaf-nosed bat was the symbol of the city in the classical Mayan period (fifth to ninth century CE), and many bat sculptures have been found in the city's ruins, one of which is both fearsome and noticeably priapic. Today, some cities wish to align themselves with bats not because they strike fear into the hearts of enemies but because they indicate a tolerant, benevolent city where difference is accepted. The Congress Avenue Bridge in Austin, Texas, is home to the world's largest urban colony of bats. Reconstruction of the bridge in 1980 unwittingly created an ideal roosting spot, and bats began to move in by the thousands. While some locals wanted

the bats eradicated or at least relocated, scientist and tireless bat campaigner Merlin Tuttle brought Bat Conservation International to town, making the city the official headquarters of the organization. Tuttle argued in his inimitable way that bats are not dangerous but 'really shy and winsome creatures who have just had bad press'.[66] 'Winsome' is not a term often used by scientists, but then, not many scientists are called Merlin. Education and advocacy won over the public and the bats were not only protected but became a draw for locals and tourists alike. Austin now has a civic sculpture of a bat in flight and an annual 'Bat Fest', which sees the bridge packed with stalls and music stages. T-shirts, mugs, caps and all manner of memorabilia style Austin as a proud bat city, in keeping with its mantra: 'Keep Austin Weird'.

There are bat festivals across the United States, Japan and Europe. In Australia several cities are home to large colonies of flying foxes, but while these add local colour, no other city has adopted the bat as its official mascot or held a festival in their honour. Flying foxes are moving to cities as their native habitats are encroached upon and as cities' temperatures rise (known as the urban heat island effect).[67] Flying foxes were only occasional visitors to Melbourne until 1986, when a few intrepid individuals overwintered in the Royal Botanic Gardens. A colony was born, and it grew to 30,000 bats by 2003, appropriate to a city where a major 'founding father' was named John Batman (there are Batman streets all over Melbourne).[68] The Botanic Gardens, however, were not happy with the destruction of historic and protected trees, so a three-year project was initiated to relocate the colony to the banks of the Yarra River, where it has remained ever since.[69]

Sydney has had similar issues with flying foxes in its Botanical Gardens. Despite the bats being a tourist attraction (since they hang from the trees like the most photogenic and exotic fruits imaginable), the bats were evicted with a combination of noise pollution and bags of python dung. Bats continue to haunt the skies of Sydney at sunset, as they do in Brisbane; most recently, they have set up camp in Adelaide. This does not, contrary to appearances, mean that the bats are thriving; unfortunately, the opposite is true. Humans have destroyed so much of bats' native habitat that now bats are being forced into closer proximity with human populations. This is a global problem for bats, as we shall see in the next chapter. So while bats have been celebrated as useful and desirable, and, in enlightened pockets of the world, as the ultimate signifiers of fortune, their own fortunes continue to hang in the balance.

4 The Beleaguered Bat: Depredation, Disease and Death

In the era now widely known as the Anthropocene, global biodiversity is plummeting; some commentators call this the sixth mass extinction event. In spite of bats' diversity and range, up to 25 per cent of bat species are considered threatened.[1] For many of the planet's fauna, including bats, habitat loss is a major threat. As human beings continue to encroach on wild spaces, development and deforestation leave fewer available niches for species that have co-evolved with endemic flora. Many bat species require specific roosting temperatures, which is why some caves are colonized and some are not. The exploitation of natural resources, military operations and other human incursions into habitats can cause abandonment of roosting sites and severely compromise bats' abilities to overwinter and reproduce.

Even guano extraction may disturb cave populations unless carefully regulated, while cave ecosystems often depend upon the guano as a source of nutrients.[2] According to those who extract guano at Bracken Cave, however, if it wasn't regularly removed, the cave, almost 20 m deep in dung, would fill up to the roof. The bats, of course, would vacate long before this took place. Even so, in deference to the bats, guano is only extracted when they have made their annual migrations elsewhere.[3]

Less obvious intrusions into habitat such as noise and light pollution can still compromise bats' feeding and migration

One of the most endangered animals on the planet, the Seychelles sheath-tail bat, of which there are only 100 remaining.

patterns. In the long term climate change may be the death knell for some species, while in the short term many bats are subject to human violence and eradication because they are seen as pests, carriers of disease or simply sources of food. Even when humans don't consciously harm or kill bats, chiropteran deaths are often the collateral damage of our anthropocentric lifestyles. Increased use of pesticides not only reduces the availability of food for insectivores, but can create a harmful toxic build-up in the bats themselves. Thousands of Australian bentwing bats died from DDT poisoning before that pesticide was outlawed in 1987.[4] Additionally, introduced predators devastate the balance of delicate ecosystems, making it harder for communities of bats to remain healthy and populous. The Christmas Island pipistrelle is now extinct owing to the predations of introduced insects and snakes. Only a photo remains, dated January 2009, of the four members of the last known colony, as well as a heartbreaking recording of the pipistrelle's echolocation call, available on YouTube as the sobering 'sound of extinction'.[5] Scientists and conservationists who came to capture the last bats for preservation and breeding

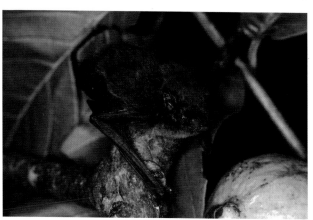

The Christmas
Island pipistrelle,
RIP.

found themselves in the devastating position of witnessing the very last member of the species flying – alone.[6]

Even when a species appears to be populous, it may in fact be in decline. Australian flying foxes are being driven into cities by the destruction of their natural habitat, where they raid orchards and private gardens because their preferred source of sustenance, flowering eucalypts, are no longer adequately available. In many states farmers and orchardists are licensed to cull flying fox populations, creating what has been referred to as a 'pteropucidal black hole' – that is, a deadly vortex which sucks in fruit bats or Pteropodidae, as their struggle for survival in a dramatically altered world is punishable by death.[7] And it is not just shooting that these bats face but a constant threat of eviction. Colony dispersal is practised anywhere in Australia where flying foxes congregate too close to humans, who dislike their noise, smell,

Attempted flying fox dispersal in Charters Towers, Queensland, with a 'fogging' machine. Other methods included water canons and helicopter buzzing.

droppings and reputation for spreading disease. In 2013 in Charters Towers, Queensland, the local council spent $80,000 on an attempted dispersal of flying foxes, using fireworks, smoke machines, paintball guns, water cannons and helicopters to 'buzz' the camp.[8] Within a year, newspaper headlines acknowledged that none of this had made any difference, and that, owing to a lack of food and water in their natural habitats, flying foxes had returned to Queensland cities in 'plague proportions'.[9] The use of such incendiary language as 'plague' highlights people's worst fears about bats, which have been speculated to be reservoirs in the spread of a number of zoonotic, or animal-to-human trans-missible, diseases. SARS, Hendra, Lyssavirus (and other forms of rabies), Menangle, Nipah and Marburg have all had their dreaded names linked to the animals. Most recently and perhaps most deadly, an outbreak of Ebola in 2014 in West Africa again spot-lighted bats as disease carriers, though the latest evidence points in other directions. All these diseases, with the exception of rabies, are asymptomatic in bats, posing interesting questions about chiropteran immunity which may actually end up being beneficial to humans.

The major reservoirs for rabies are members of Carnivora, most notoriously dogs, but also foxes, raccoons and skunks. Bats too can host the disease, but apart from vampire bats, which make a habit of biting larger animals, very few bats infected with rabies pass it on.[10] While 95 per cent of rabies deaths occur in Asia and Africa and almost all of these are caused by dog bites, bat rabies in Latin America is still an issue, and while human mortal-ity rates are low, thousands of livestock meet grisly ends due to the predations of vampire bats. But herein lies the quandary: the populations of *Desmodus rotundus*, used to feeding on small native mammals, exploded with the introduction of large, docile Euro-pean livestock. Humans have upset the natural balance, and now vampire bats are responsible for more than u.s.$30 million worth of livestock damage annually, so culling is widely practised. Recent research, however, demonstrates that culling vampires does not lower the rate of rabies infection: if anything, it makes the disease more common by making the beleaguered bat populations more susceptible, as we shall see.[11]

The Hendra virus is named for the Brisbane suburb where it was first reported in 1994. It is an acute respiratory disease found in horses, transmissible to humans, but originating in fruit bats.[12] After extensive surveillance of more than forty animal species in Queensland, Hendra virus was discovered in all four flying fox species, including in historic archived samples, demonstrating that Hendra is not a new virus; that is, not new to the bats, which have always lived there. Conversely, studies showed that stresses to the bats boosted the numbers testing positive for the disease. In 2011 summer floods and cyclones in Queensland saw increased numbers of malnourished and immunocompromised bats, and samples of populations indicated that up to 30 per cent were carrying the virus, compared with the usual rate of around 7 per cent.[13] However, it is important to acknowledge that Hendra has never been transmitted from a flying fox to a human, in spite of the close contact they share with bat carers and researchers.

While only four humans and fewer than a hundred horses have died due to Hendra, regular horse outbreaks continued to be reported until the introduction of a vaccine in 2012. Unfortunately the outbreak of the related Nipah virus in Malaysia between 1998 and 1999 took a more dramatic toll on livestock. This disease was transmissible from pigs to humans, and 105 people died while more than a million pigs were put to death to stop its spread.[14] While fruit bats were pinpointed as the problem, it was the pig farms that were encroaching into the bats' native habitat. This real-life scenario was exploited in the Hollywood medical thriller

Contagion (dir. Steven Soderbergh, 2011), which dramatizes the spread of a fictional airborne disease that kills 26 million people worldwide. In the finale we see a spliced-together sequence of events, the cause and effect of how and where the virus started. First, a mining company's bulldozer ploughs into a stand of palm trees somewhere in Hong Kong, evicting fruit bats. One of the scattered bats finds a bunch of bananas to feed on, but drops a chunk of fruit, mid-flight, into an open-air pig pen. The pigs are then sold for meat, and the chef preparing the meal wipes, but doesn't wash, his bloody hands before meeting and greeting Gwyneth Paltrow, an executive from the mining company that knocked down the palm tree: Paltrow turns out to be 'patient zero'. As one of the scientists searching for an antidote puts it, 'Somewhere in the world the wrong pig met up with the wrong bat,' but it was global development that was the ultimate culprit. Some scientists surmise that the major driver in the emergence of zoonotic diseases is not 'dirty' or 'dangerous' animals, but human population expansion into wildlife habitats.[15] Bat scientist and advocate Merlin Tuttle remains sceptical, however, given the fact that throughout human history until very recently, we have shared our dwellings with bats, and that compared to a host of other dangerous animals, bats have one of the 'finest safety records' when it comes to co-habiting with humans.[16]

One of the more visceral moments in *Contagion* features the waiter who picked up Paltrow's infected martini glass staggering through the wet markets of Hong Kong, coughing and spluttering as all kinds of live caged animals and cuts of meat are proffered for sale. So disoriented is he that he walks into traffic and is immediately hit by a truck. The real-life SARS virus originated in the wet markets of southern China, where an incendiary mix of fresh meat, produce, livestock and wild animals provided the perfect meeting place for host-hungry viruses. This particular outbreak was traced to masked palm civets, and consequently, more than 10,000 of these animals were killed in Guangdong Province, but further studies speculated that while civets, raccoon dogs and cats harbour the virus, it might have originated in horse-shoe bats, though to date these suggestions are far from proven. Unfortunately there were almost eight hundred human fatalities, and thanks to air travel, the disease dispersed beyond China's borders, infecting people in Taiwan, Hong Kong, Singapore, Canada and elsewhere before it was finally contained.[17] While these numbers are still minuscule compared to other human killers such as cancer and heart disease, fear of a pandemic has captured the popular imagination, leading to an outpouring of research funding and the hunt for scapegoats (or bats, as the case may be).

Parallels have been drawn between Chinese wet markets and the emergence of SARS, and the African bushmeat trade and HIV-like viruses.[18] More recently, the terrifying and tragic Ebola epidemic which claimed the lives of almost 11,000 people in Guinea, Liberia and Sierra Leone early in 2014 saw warnings issued against the consumption of bushmeat of all kinds. While there are many factors affecting the spread of zoonoses in parts of Africa, this outbreak was almost immediately blamed on straw-coloured fruit bats. However, the 'index case', a two-year-old boy from the small village of Meliandou in Guinea who first became ill, had no known contact with either a fruit bat or with any other human who had. When this was pointed out subsequent investigators blamed insect-eating free-tailed bats (*Mops condylurus*) instead, reporting that the two-year-old had played in or near a hollow tree occupied by these bats. The bats were burned in their roost, despite the fact that evidence was slim, and teenage boys who reportedly had often caught and eaten the free-tailed bats had not gotten sick. More than a dozen bat species were sampled from the area, and none showed evidence of Ebola infection.

In the coverage of the tragedy, headlines were quick to associate bats with the deadly haemhorrhagic fever. Yet a closer reading of the articles reveals that scientists and journalists use precautionary language such as 'maybe', 'might' and 'likely' when linking bats to the outbreak. Two years on from the Ebola outbreak, virologists remain unconvinced that bats were indeed the culprits. Ebola expert Dr Daniel Bausch of the World Health Organization stated categorically, 'no one has ever grown an Ebola virus from a bat.'[19] Even those experimentally infected with the Ebola virus show no evidence of viral shedding.[20] Virologist Jens Kuhn of the u.s. National Institute of Allergy and Infectious Diseases suggests that insects or even fungi may be potential sources of the deadly virus.[21] If aquatic insects were to blame, the extermination of insectivorous bats would have a deleterious effect on the control of future outbreaks. This particular Ebola outbreak was one example of many in which sensationalism led to harmful speciesism and unwarranted reprisal killings.

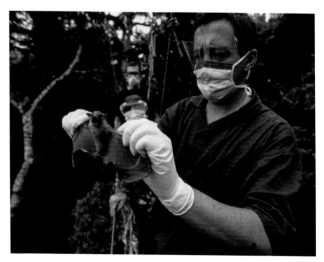

Bat caught for Ebola testing in Ivory Coast, Africa.

Richard Preston's 1994 non-fiction thriller *The Hot Zone* became a best-seller by engaging the public's fear of pandemics. The book chronicles the origins of several zoonotic diseases in parts of Africa, with the opening story featuring a pseudonymous Charles Monet, French caretaker of a Kenyan sugar factory. Monet loves animals – he is always feeding monkeys and caring for sick birds. He also loves wilderness, and sets about exploring the scenery of Mt Elgon with a local female companion. Together they visit Kitum, a massive cave where elephants are known to congregate. In other words, as with the 2014 outbreak of Ebola, there are countless potential vectors for a deadly disease; Marburg, in this case, ends up killing the hapless Frenchman and his partner. The floor of Kitum Cave is coated with green slime – fruit bats' guano – while hundreds of bat eyes, 'like red jewels', look down upon the couple from the ceiling of the cave.[22] The cave is in fact a petrified rainforest, where ancient logs had transformed into opal and chert, surrounded by white, needle-like crystals that the author compares, appropriately in this medical horror, to hypodermic syringes. The narrative is a strange mixture of fear and seduction as the lovers penetrate deeper into the cave where Monet finds a 'velvety mass of bats' excreting black guano as opposed to the green slime he found at the mouth of the cave: these bats are clearly insectivores.[23] Preston wonders if Monet had been compelled to touch the black ooze, or indeed, if he and his lady friend had disrobed and made love in the depths of the cave. Whatever took place, within a couple of weeks Monet is vomiting blood and his eyes have become fiery red jewels like those attributed to the bats. Preston's story is a terrifying update on the vampire tale's mix of sensuality and contagion, a new kind of *Dracula* minus the morality: horror for a godless age.

Near the book's conclusion, the author himself travels to Kitum Cave to see where the virus originated and which animal might have been the host. There is a surprising streak of black humour in his description of bat guano as 'a spinach-green paste speckled with grey blobs, which reminded me of Oysters Rockefeller'.[24] Later he indulges in some rather more doleful musing, wondering if the earth is 'mounting an immune response against the human species' and AIDS is 'the revenge of the rainforest'.[25]

When Preston travels to Kitum, there are too many potential animal vectors to choose from for a conclusive ending. However, the book was written in 1994, and by 2009, scientists were declaring they had found Marburg antibodies in Egyptian fruit bats (which, however, only proves exposure to a disease, and not that the animal is a carrier).[26] The spread of this information may have had something to do with the horrific shooting of up to 5,000 of these bats out of a colony of 7,000 in Lebanon in 2012. The carnage was discovered by Dr Mounir Abi-Said, founder of Animal Encounter, a Lebanese wildlife conservation group. One year later, Abi-Said reported that, thanks to the public education projects he initiated, and the watchful eye of local police, the cave was again flourishing as a roosting site.[27] While all of this was taking place, Middle Eastern Respiratory Syndrome (MERS) emerged in late 2012 and was tentatively traced back to the Egyptian tomb bat, with the camel as the intermediary carrier or 'amplifier' species. As with much reporting on issues connecting bats and disease, the headlines tell half the story. 'Deadly coronavirus found in bats' seems conclusive, but the subtitle is less certain: 'Discovery hints at virus's source,' while the article as a whole demonstrates that scientists are actually in disagreement over this issue.[28] Still later reports failed to link bats to MERS at all. Bats are not alone in falling victim to media sensationalism, but they endure more than their fair share of speciesist scapegoating.

So why are bats so often implicated in the spread of zoonotic diseases? Is it lingering prejudice, or are they really exemplary hosts? One school of scientific thought suggests that it is simply a question of numbers – there are so many species of bat, so widespread throughout the globe and in some of those environments in extraordinarily high densities, that certain instances of disease must become inevitable. Bats also live longer than other small mammals, creating a stable reservoir for diseases, while flying great lengths for foraging, with some species seasonally migrating over long distances and potentially transporting pathogens with them.[29]

Other scientists believe that it is not just a question of numbers, but that bats are indeed different and special – and consequently their physiologies and lifestyles need to be studied carefully if we are to grasp what predisposes them to being vectors of disease.[30] Analysis of bat genomes suggests that antiviral surveillance mechanisms in bats are perpetually on high alert. This is possibly related to their capability for flight, in which bats' metabolic rate is boosted to much higher levels than when at rest. These sustained energy bursts would create stress and cellular damage if not quickly detected and repaired, which is exactly what bat genes seem to be capable of doing. Intriguingly, while in humans and other vertebrates, viral infections trigger the production of proteins known as interferon, bats themselves have fewer interferon genes than other mammals, yet they appear able to tolerate continual interferon activation.[31] Viruses fail to gain hold in such hypervigilant immune systems, and while bats may prove to carry antibodies of various diseases, they are rarely capable of infecting other animals. If we understood what enables bats' immune systems to counteract dangerous viruses, we could apply these lessons to the development of effective vaccines.[32] Studying bats might even hold creative solutions to broader problems, including increasing resistance to viruses, bacteria and fungi.[33] The super immunity of bats may be the key to preventing the pandemics of the future.

While bats may be impervious to a range of potentially devastating viruses, there is one disease which has wreaked havoc among the bat populations of North America. White-nose syndrome, or WNS, is the common name given to *Pseudogymnoascus destructans*, a cold-loving fungus that emerged in the northeastern United States in 2006. The fungus attacks seven different species of cave-hibernating bats and forms a conspicuous white growth, primarily on the face, ears and wings, while it infiltrates underlying tissues.[34]

Symptoms include abnormal behaviour among hibernating bats, such as restlessness, movement and even daytime flights during winter, which means that bats burn up their fat reserves and essentially die of starvation.[35] It is estimated that a staggering 90 per cent of bats in the affected regions have been wiped out – well over 6 million at the time of writing. Following the disease is enormously disheartening, as it has moved north into Canada and west and south across the United States, with more and more

Little brown bats infected with White-nose syndrome, New York State, 2007.

White-nose syndrome arouses bats from hibernation when there are no insects to eat – they subsequently die of starvation. Greg Turner of the Pennsylvania Game Commission discovers a cluster of dead bats in the snow.

states reporting its presence in their bat populations. By 2017, 33 states and five Canadian provinces were affected, including, most disturbingly, Washington in the Pacific Northwest, the opposite side of the continent to the disease's origin, and Texas in the southwest, home to the largest concentration of bat populations.[36] WNS has already been discovered in some species endemic to Europe, but has not had any associated fatalities, leading to speculation that the disease may have originated there and been transported to the U.S. via a human carrier (the first infection on record was at a 'show cave' in New York State). In this instance it seems that humans may have been the disease vectors, bringing the devastating infection with them on that historically destructive viral highway from Europe to the Americas.

If the spread of WNS doesn't slow down, the little brown bat, once a very common species, could become extinct in the northeast in less than twenty years,[37] which would severely unbalance ecosystems. There is, however, a glimmer of hope: despite massive

Desmodus rotundus, the common vampire bat, feeds on a chicken in French Guiana.

losses, small pockets of bats have survived in caves where infection was present. These bats appear to be resistant to the disease and, if they continue to breed successfully, will begin to repopulate the areas devastated by WNS.

In spite of staggering global death tolls, selective killing of certain bat populations is still rubber-stamped by governments in various countries. Vampire bats are an obvious target; their populations are culled by the use of anticoagulant chemicals such as warfarin, spread onto the coats of so-called 'Judas bats'. These bats are then re-released into colonies where, being highly social creatures, they are groomed by other bats, thus exposing them to the deadly poison. Vampire bat specialist Bill Schutt acknowledges an element of poetic justice in this tale – these bats, after all, bleed their victims via anticoagulants in their saliva, and warfarin is an anticoagulant used to treat thrombosis in humans.[38]

Yet in small mammals such as rats and bats, this paste leads to a violent haemhorrhagic death akin to those dramatically described in *The Hot Zone*, and may actually exacerbate the spread of disease. Colonies that are periodically culled demonstrate higher rates of exposure to rabies: 12 per cent as opposed to 7 per cent in colonies where culling never took place. This may be because the grooming bats are always adults, who are more likely to have acquired resistance to rabies. Juveniles, who do not groom other bats and are more susceptible to developing rabies, become proportionally more numerous and thus disturb the balance of the roost, encouraging the spread of disease.[39]

Similarly for flying foxes in Australia, stresses on colonies, including state-sanctioned shooting by permitted farmers, make the bats more likely to be carriers of both Hendra and Lyssavirus. For the time being, however, the demands of fruit farmers to protect their livelihoods with shotguns outweighs the messages from conservationists. Under a Labour government, the state of Queensland had first banned the electrocution of flying foxes in 2001 and

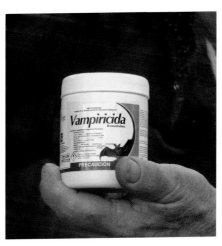

No garlic or wooden stakes; Latin American ranchers use warfarin creams like this one to kill vampire bats, though its use is controversial.

then the shooting of these animals in 2008; both methods of crop protection were ruled to be inhumane. The year 2012 ushered in a conservative coalition between the Liberal and National parties which overturned the laws, allowing farmers to resume the shooting of bats.[40] In peculiarly poor taste, this change to the law was announced on 7 September, Threatened Species Day in Australia, which commemorates the death of the last Tasmanian tiger at the Hobart zoo in 1936. Ironically, two of the four species of flying foxes that orchardists are mandated to kill are actually listed as threatened species (the grey-headed flying fox and the spectacled flying fox). Many bats shot on the wing are merely wounded and thus doomed to die a painful, lingering death. Baby bats who cling to their mothers when very young are collateral damage, condemned to starve to death, while those old enough to stay back at the camp, yet still too young to fly or feed themselves, will meet the same sorry end.[41] Unfortunately, commercial fruiting season coincides with the birthing season for flying fox pups, meaning

'Don't Shoot Bats' protest takes place in Queensland, Australia, where farmers can obtain permits to shoot bats in order to protect fruit crops.

that a large proportion of those bats shot on the wing will be mothers with mouths to feed. The Grey Cross, an Australian humanitarian organization that asks farmers not to shoot bats, hangs grey crosses upside down, in deference to the bats' sooty colouring and reverse orientation, in trees near the sites of these massacres.

The Australian 'Grey Cross' campaign memorializes locations where flying foxes have been killed.

In the fruiting season from 2014–15, all fourteen requests for 'Damage Mitigation Permits' in the state of Queensland were granted, allowing the permit holders to shoot a combined total of 10,580 bats.[42] While it might have been superstition, cruelty for cruelty's sake or fear of infectious diseases that saw 5,000 fruit bats lose their lives in a Lebanon cave on that fateful day in 2012, it could equally have been angry farmers who were tired of bats ransacking their crops. Had those farmers lived in Queensland, their bullets would have received an official stamp of approval.

Meanwhile, the state government of New South Wales, which has also allowed culling of flying foxes, is phasing out its shooting permits and instead subsidizing suitable netting, which is more expensive but far more effective in the long-term maintenance of orchards against the depredations of bats.

Australian scientist and pro-bat activist Tim Pearson made a tongue-in-cheek but nonetheless poignant comparison between flying foxes and refugees, both of whom are regarded with suspicion by middle Australia. Warming up in front of his audience for his talk at TEDX Canberra in 2013, he made knowing comments about 'a group in our society who's not very popular', noting that these misunderstood folk 'work the nightshift' doing a critical job that no one acknowledges: 'They are at best ignored, sometimes vilified, quite often even actively persecuted.'[43] Once he has outed bats as the real subject of his lecture, Pearson points out that flying foxes are often literally refugees, fleeing from harassment, violence and the destruction of their homes. Pearson believes that instead of making bats' lives more difficult, we should be rolling out the red carpet and treating them like the 'environmental superstars' they really are, for their exemplary role in reforestation.

Diane Ackerman undertook a lengthy interview with the great scientist, photographer and founder of Bat Conservation International Merlin Tuttle about the indiscriminate killing of bats. For Tuttle, one of the tragedies that perpetrators may not even be aware of is that some bats live for more than thirty years, so it's 'not like killing a roach'.[44] Tuttle ruminates on the slow reproduction of bats, figuring that if you took a pair of meadow mice and gave them everything they and their progeny needed to survive, theoretically there could be a million mice by the end of the year, whereas the same opportunity given to a pair of bats would yield a grand total of three bats, meaning that large-scale culls are enormously difficult for bat populations to recover from. Tuttle laments that in his time he has known of caves where literally millions of bats have been wiped out in a day. He considers anti-bat hysteria utterly misguided, noting that statistically more people die in America from bee stings, dog attacks or having vending machines fall on them than from bat-transmissable diseases.[45]

Not only are bats wrongfully accused of misdeeds, but it is often the *wrong bats* that get punished for the supposed crimes of others. The discovery of rabies in vampire bats in Trinidad in the 1940s resulted in the deaths of thousands of non-blood-feeding species. Dynamite, flamethrowers and poison gas were indiscriminately enlisted against all kinds of bats, and the success of this programme saw it followed in post-Second World War Brazil, and later still in Venezuela, where nearly a million bats were killed annually from 1964 to 1966.[46] The mistaken identification of innocent blossom bats as bloodthirsty vampires has a long history. In the early 1800s Johann Baptist von Spix made a triumphant return from Brazil to the Bavarian Academy of Sciences with thousands of specimens, including *Glossophaga soricina*, a pollen-eating bat he declared to be 'a very cruel blood-sucker'. Spix was certain that the animal's bristly tongue, adapted for collecting pollen from flowers, was a tool for brutalizing flesh wounds inflicted by the bat's impossibly dainty teeth.[47] If this hummingbird-like creature could be accused of blood-sucking, imagine what was made of the several species of bats with large canines, despite the fact that these teeth were designed to pierce nothing more sanguineous than thick-skinned figs. Unsurprisingly, these bats were given portentous vampiric names by nineteenth-century taxonomists, such as *Vampyrodes*, *Vampyressa*, *Vampyrops* and *Vampyriscus*,[48] each of which is worthy of a comic-book villain. Owing to misinformation, bat killing continues today in Latin America, where until relatively recently the words for 'bat' and 'vampire' were interchangeable. Tuttle tells the tale of a Mexican philanthropist who

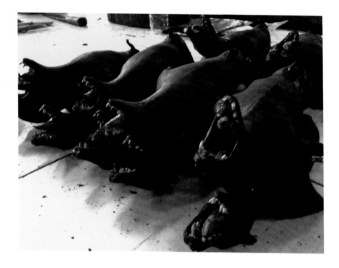

Bats as bushmeat, here in the Tomohon market, Indonesia.

joined Bat Conservation International's board of directors in 1995 and whose secretary updated his résumé to show that he was now a trustee of Vampire Conservation International.[49] In addition to vampire hysteria, there have been localized outbreaks of an even more bizarre panic surrounding the mythical chupacabra figure. Chupacabras are creatures that may be half-man, half-bat; they kill animals and potentially people by complete desanguination.[50] The chupacabra myth seems to spring up with more intensity at times of economic hardship, and many bat caves have been burned out as a result of this seasonal mass hallucination.

There are tragic ironies and hypocrisies in operation when it comes to the misfortune of bats. They are accused of being carriers of disease, and yet they are dying in their millions of a disease that was possibly spread by, and causes no harm to, humans. They are reviled for the fact that a very small minority of them are blood feeders, yet people all over the world happily feast on bats. In parts of Africa, Asia and many Pacific and Caribbean islands, bats suffer human predation; for some cultural groups, the eating of bats is thought to have medicinal value, while for many Micronesians a fruit bat is considered a delicacy, traditionally eaten at celebrations.[51] Fruit bat recipes even turn up in Western cookbooks, as with the Victorian-era publications of Mrs Lance Rawson, who advocated that white settlers of Australia get creative with the country's natural bounty. Following the eating practices of Aboriginals, but with a European twist, Rawson wrote that flying fox was 'excellent eating' during the fruiting season, but warned would-be bat eaters that when that season was over, the bats took on a 'peculiar flavour' from a particular flower or leaf they ate when there was no fruit around.[52] In order to eat the flying fox, its wings have to be disposed of and, once cleaned, the whitish de-winged bat looks for all the world like a skinned fowl. Now it can be 'stuffed with breadcrumbs and herbs or mashed potatoes, and roasted or boiled', for a 'young flying fox, split like a Spatch Cock and grilled, makes a capital breakfast dish'.[53] When the Western revival of natural and native foods started in the 1970s, a recipe for fruit bat

Fruit bat soup, a delicacy in many Caribbean countries.

131

soup, featuring spring onions, soy sauce and coconut cream, appeared in the *New York Times Natural Foods Cookbook*, 'on the off-chance that a reader may find himself in Micronesia'.[54]

Such First World dalliances with native foods are an exotic novelty. In other parts of the world, bats are hunted opportunistically along with various wild animals as necessary sources of protein in otherwise limited diets. But although bat eating, apart from pushing some species towards extinction, has been associated with the spread of zoonotic diseases, bat advocate Tuttle is keen to point out that if bats posed anywhere near as big a disease threat as often claimed, the millions of people who eat them, as well as those extracting guano from caves, should be in big trouble, reaching epidemic proportions by now.

Whether for the sake of conservation or human safety, bat hunting is often outlawed, but poorly policed. The cost of bats being sold for consumption varies wildly depending on how effective the law enforcement is, and how much danger the poacher has undertaken. In the Philippines, where there is minimal implementation of hunting regulations, a large fruit bat can be sold for as little as 60 U.S. cents, while in the Mariana Islands, where poaching is strictly punished, a single bat can fetch U.S.$100.[55] Higher prices are their own incentive, while lower prices mean more killing is required to make a profit. Either way, the bats lose.

One instance of bat-eating has been linked to disease, in this case profound neurological disorders among the Chamorro people of Guam. The local bats, a traditional delicacy, feed on the fruits of cycad plants which contain high levels of neurotoxins. Scientists including Oliver Sacks theorized that it was the islanders' bat diet that was leading to the debilitating disease responsible for the deaths of many Chamorro. The incidence of disease decreased only when, with their own flying foxes hunted to near extinction, the Chamorro started to import flying fox meat from Samoa, which didn't have the same cycad plant population. The hypothesis is still controversial; nevertheless, it is hoped that further study of this particular island's tragic historical malady may shed light on degenerative neurological diseases the world over.[56]

It is not only the Chamorro's fondness for fruit bat meat that brought these animals to the brink of extinction. The accidental introduction of the Asian-Australasian brown tree snake around 1950 has been devastating for native bat, bird and lizard populations on Guam.[57] Island populations are always the hardest hit by introduced species. In New Zealand, introduced mice, rats, stoats and feral cats are a huge problem for bats: one of only three endemic species of Chiroptera hasn't been seen since 1967 and is thought to be extinct. Many snakes, birds of prey and even some spiders feed on bats. But these are natural predators which have co-evolved with bats and do not pose any serious threat to the sustainability of bat populations. Introduced predators cause much more damage, as do domestic and feral cats. Worldwide, cats kill an estimated 250,000 bats per year.[58] Domestic cats who do not need bats for nutrition will hunt them for sport: since cats can hear their echolocation calls, they must make a tantalizing squeaky toy. Unfortunately, feline fun wounds bats so badly that they either die or fall victim to secondary predators, such as foxes in the UK.[59] Feral cats hunt bats for food, as evidenced by a cat trapped and killed in rural New Zealand in 2010. Over seven days this cat had killed a total of 102 short-tailed bats, a species listed as 'vulnerable'. The euthanized cat was pictured lying next to the depredated remains of some of the bats it didn't quite manage to digest. So, there is a definitive answer to the question the adventurous Alice poses as she plunges down the rabbit hole, wondering if she will end up in Australia or New Zealand (the 'antipathies'). Wishing her cat Dinah could be with her, she realizes that as she is currently airborne, Dinah wouldn't

be able to catch any mice, but she might be able to catch a bat. Only, Alice isn't sure if cats eat bats, and as she falls ever deeper into the hole she asks herself, 'Do cats eat bats? Do cats eat bats?'[60] Unfortunately, for bat-lovers and cat-lovers alike, they most certainly do. In the topsy-turvy world of Wonderland, Alice also asks, 'do bats eat cats?' and while the answer to this is not on record, there are certainly examples of tit-for-tat eating in the bat kingdom: there are frog-eating bats, but then there are also bat-eating toads, as attested to by particularly macabre online image galleries.

When bats are not the victims of direct killing by people or the predators they wittingly and unwittingly bring with them, a less tangible though more insidious threat exists which has the potential to be the most devastating of all. Climate change in its many and varied manifestations threatens bats all over the globe in different ways. Scientists are hesitant to link White-nose syndrome to the fluctuating temperatures of North American winters, but there is little doubt that on the other side of the

Feral cat caught in the Rangataua Conservation Area of New Zealand, with remnants of the endangered bats it had killed and eaten.

This strange hybrid creature is a product of nature, not photoshop or Surrealist collage. Peruvian park ranger Yufani Olaya snapped a photo of an unfortunate bat being eaten by a cane toad in 2011, and it became an instant Internet sensation.

Dead flying foxes gathered together for disposal in the heat stress event at Bomaderry, New South Wales, Australia, in January 2013.

world in Australia, heat waves with record highs of over 40°c have decimated flying fox populations. In extreme states of stress, the bats urinate on themselves in an effort to cool down, while in some cases volunteers squirt overheated bats with water pistols. Often, however, assistance doesn't arrive or comes too late. In a debilitating heat wave in early January 2014, at least 45,500 fruit bats were reported to be 'dropping out of the sky' in Queensland. Dead bodies littered the ground, and the stench was overwhelming. Council workers removed wheelie bins full of bodies, while wildlife carers suddenly had over a thousand orphaned flying foxes to foster.[61] Because flying foxes live in colonies, it is easier to determine the impact of extreme heat events on the species as a whole than on species that live more solitary lifestyles. They are excellent 'bioindicators': twenty-first-century canaries in the Gaian coal mine, telling us that life is literally getting too hot to handle. And if hibernating bats taking daylight flights or sun-loving bats overcooking aren't scary enough signs of uncertain times, just imagine what will happen when rising temperatures increase the range of vampire bats, who are intolerant of cold.

In a cruelly ironic twist, one of the best ways of generating renewable energy to alleviate such dramatic climate conditions is *also* the enemy of bats. Wind turbines offer a promising alternative to fossil fuels, but unfortunately they also cause untold bat deaths: over a million in the U.S. and Canada in a single year.[62] So why do bats, who are extraordinary navigators, fall foul of these blades? Bats are attracted to tall objects that may resemble potential roosts in tree snags. Turbines are also commonly located on ridgetops where swarms of insects congregate in late summer. Many

A hoary bat found dead under a wind turbine in the United States.

Orphaned flying foxes are given tiny dummies and swaddled in blankets, as they would be tightly wrapped in their mother's wings. When mothers fly out for nightly foraging, young flying foxes come for the ride, attaching to the nipple and clinging to their mothers' fur with their toes.

unfortunate bats are likely just attempting to feed in traditional areas of insect abundance. As they get closer to the turbines, the change in air pressure caused by the speedy rotation of the blades ruptures the bats' internal organs. There are solutions: by not spinning turbine blades during periods of low wind on calm nights (a process known as 'feathering'), fatalities could be dramatically reduced. In many cases, feathering may only be necessary during three months out of the year. Since little energy is generated at such times only about 1 per cent of generated energy would be lost. Additionally, researchers are also investigating acoustic deterrents and ultraviolet lighting as alternative means to keep bats away from these death traps.[63] Unfortunately, many companies continue to ignore new findings that could prevent kills, and this likely will continue until more people and organizations express concern for the bats and birds that fall victim to turbines.

News isn't all bad for bats. Issues such as White-nose Syndrome, heat waves and introduced predators have increased public awareness of the plight of these important creatures. People who might once have found bats creepy are more than happy to post videos of orphaned baby bats on their Facebook pages, being wrapped in swaddling cloths (see the Youtube clip 'Baby Bat Burritos'), sucking on outsize dummies or having their cheeks stuffed with grapes. Bats have gone from being dark and scary to cute, but it didn't happen overnight. The change in public attitudes is thanks in large part to the incredible photography of Tuttle, who since the late 1970s has been taking action shots of bats on the wing as well as portraits that make his chiropteran sitters look like stately Victorian gentlemen. Tuttle founded Bat Conservation International in 1982, and it is testament to his artistry that so many public attitudes have improved; his stunning photographs have made bats a global cause célèbre.[64] Bats have also become huge news in children's literature; scanning any library database for books on bats will yield numerous story books with batty characters, all written within the last twenty years. Children are routinely recruited as bat advocates by educators who know that parents' attitudes are harder to change. And, as we shall see in the next chapter, even artists are taking up the issue of bat conservation. Bats, beleaguered or not, are 'so hot right now'.

Despite his successes, Tuttle fears a potential reversal in public opinion due to sensationalist associations of bats with disease. He now provides regular alerts regarding misleading or untrue coverage of bats through his newly founded organization, Merlin Tuttle's Bat Conservation, where 'bat fans' can subscribe to receive 'bat flashes' any time, anywhere, bats are being unfairly targeted.

5 Potent Totem:
The Bat in Art and Philosophy

We have explored the dazzling diversity of bats, witnessed the disdain they have induced, as well as the delight, and acknowledged some of the threats bats face globally today. In the hopes that creative and visual thinking will sow the seeds for a reappraisal of bats in the popular imagination, this chapter examines the totemic qualities which endear bats to artists and philosophers. The anthropologist Claude Lévi-Strauss once famously said of totemic classifications that animals were selected because they were not only 'good to eat' but 'good to think' (with).[1] Henry David Thoreau prefigured Lévi-Strauss's creaturely logic when he wrote that all animals are beasts of burden, for they are all made to 'carry some portion of our thoughts'.[2] Clearly, bats bear the burdens of our fear and misunderstanding, but other attributes have been ascribed to the bat: they even operate as strange mirrors to humanity.

Lévi-Strauss also said that a person's relationship to their totem wasn't simply a matter of 'external analogy' – of looking, or behaving superficially like something else – but must be *felt* as an internal homology or sympathy.[3] While Batman, bat clans and bat fans bedeck themselves with bat-like insignia, it is inner qualities that ultimately bespeak batness. We see intuition in the bat's uncanny ability to navigate in the dark, or finely tuned emotional intelligence in the mother bat's ability to find her unique child

Bats are emblems of sociability: here one individual Schreibers' long-fingered bat crowd-surfs over the rest.

among millions of bat babies. Bats are by and large social and familial creatures, as their large roosts attest to. In confinement, it has been noted that the common pipistrelle is therapeutic to bats of other species, and will 'comfort' sick bats by nuzzling.[4] Bats' gregarious natures make their depiction in Gothic fantasy as signifiers of lonely gloom all the less tenable. Bats may be solitary hunters, but they always come home to roost (although, as we have seen in the previous chapter, those homes may be increasingly precarious).

Bats are socially sophisticated, resembling primates, elephants and dolphins in maintaining long-term 'friendships' and sharing information and food. Some, such as Brazilian free-tails and vampires, even adopt orphans and help to feed needy individuals. Vampires must have their meals on a regular basis, but finding blood can be difficult, and not all vampires are successful every night. If a vampire misses more than a couple of meals, it will starve to death, but within close communities, unrelated females regurgitate part of their meal for a 'buddy' who has been unable to feed, although males don't share with other males, since they may be potential rivals.[5] Vampires also remember who has helped them in the past and are likely to return the favour.[6] *Desmodus* can even remember 'cheaters' who beg but don't reciprocate, because vampires, as you might expect, can also be accused of trickery: *Diaemus* mimic chicks to trick hens into allowing them to cuddle up – with unpleasant, if rarely fatal, consequences.[7] This bat will also mount a hen and bite the back of her neck, while the poor bird maintains a submissive posture as if she were being mounted by a rooster.[8] In both cases, the luckless hen is tricked by the wily bat's manipulation of her breeding instincts.

Tricksterism, a worthy quality for a clan totem, might further be glossed as flexibility, which the bat, with its compliant wings, has in spades. Bat wings are uniquely fluid compared to anything seen in the world of birds or insects, or built by human hands. This ability to take flight and exist in the airy world of ideas makes bats the perfect totem for those whose heads are in the clouds. Of course, bats are more likely to evoke emotional responses rather than calm cogitation, yet this shapeshifter can also fill the role of philosopher's muse. The ancient Greek philosopher Chaerephon was known as 'the Bat'; much later, the German naturalist Conrad Gessner explained that, 'not only does this animal not appear by day as with philosophers, but both hide and philosophize'.[9] The poet Emily Dickinson once described a bat as an 'Elate philosopher!' whose eccentricities, like those of a savant, are beneficent, while any malevolence is 'auspiciously withheld'.[10] In the inevitable collection of essays titled *Batman and Philosophy* the travails of the comic-book hero are described as a 'Nietzschean struggle to face the madness and suffering that is part of life'.[11] But it was Thomas Nagel's essay on consciousness called 'What Is It Like to Be a bat?' (1974) that cemented the relationship between bats and philosophical enquiry.

Nagel's pessimistic meditation emphasizes the impossibility of objective understanding of subjective experience, a problem which could be applied to any interspecies encounter, or indeed, encounters between individual humans. Nagel chose a bat to express his hypothesis because its sensory apparatus is so different to our own that it constitutes a 'fundamentally *alien* form of life' and therefore the answer to 'What is it like to be a bat?' is that we will never know.[12]

Nagel's text is one of the most oft-quoted works on the problem of consciousness, particularly within the field of human-animal relations, not least in J. M. Coetzee's *The Lives of Animals*. This unusual novella is built around a lecture given by the fictional novelist Elizabeth Costello, who may or may not represent Coetzee himself. Costello's lecture is about animal consciousness and animal rights and contains a discussion of Nagel's essay. Costello doesn't buy the philosopher's disavowal of interspecies empathy and understanding. As someone who makes a living from her imagination, she declares, 'If I can think my way into the existence of a being who has never existed, then I can think my way into the existence of a bat or a chimpanzee or an oyster, any being with whom I share the substrate of life.'[13] We all share in this life: 'being fully a bat is like being fully human, which is also to be full of being.'[14] According to Costello, animals, including humans, are all embodied souls, which Descartes refuted when he compared non-human animals to machines. She opposes his 'Cogito ergo sum' with what she calls 'fullness, embodiedness, the sensation of being – not a consciousness of yourself as a kind of ghostly reasoning machine thinking thoughts, but on the contrary the sensation – a heavily affective sensation – of being a body with limbs that have extension in space, of being alive to the world'.[15]

As one of four real-life respondents to Coetzee's novella, Wendy Doniger points out that before Nagel's bat essay, equine metaphors had been used to express the problem of animal minds – from Xenophanes in ancient Greece to twentieth-century anthropologists A. R. Radcliffe-Brown and Max Gluckman.[16] Doniger suggests that Nagel probably chose a bat rather than a horse 'to make the point of noncommunication more dramatic, because we don't *love* bats'. While bat lovers would disagree, Doniger continues 'we can understand horses because we love them (and, tautologically, we love them because we understand them)'.[17] This has interesting implications when we consider the hysterical accounts of the deaths of beloved horses caused by despised bats – from Quincey Morris's mare in *Dracula* to the Australian racing horses killed by the Hendra virus.

If love requires understanding, then we need better public education about bats. But some people love bats precisely *because* they are mysterious and unknowable, because their fancy flight simulates flights of fancy. Nagel, however, is not interested in imagination, stating that readers should give up any pretensions of fantasizing 'that one has webbing on one's arms, which enables one to fly around at dusk and dawn catching insects in one's mouth; that one has very poor vision, and perceives the surrounding world by a system of reflected high-frequency sound signals; and that one spends the day hanging upside down by one's feet in an attic'.[18] Such speculative reveries are only illustrative of the human perception of what it is like to be a bat, and not how the bat experiences bat-being, what Nagel charmingly refers to as 'bat phenomenology'.[19] In spite of what Nagel believes to be the impossibility of this act of empathy, he does not feel we should lazily dismiss the existence of worlds we cannot access. For Nagel, difference does not justify indifference, and he characterizes such anthropocentric thinking as 'the crudest form of cognitive dissonance'.[20]

Costello's view that both bats and humans, having bodies with extendable limbs, are able to share affective sensation contrasts strongly with Nagel's pronouncement that imagining webbing on one's arms will not get one into the mind of a bat. Yet who is to say that there isn't an internal homology or sympathy between spreading a wing membrane and stretching a human arm? Richard Morecroft, a newsreader for the Australian Broadcasting Corporation, was able to test this theory when he fostered Archie, a juvenile grey-headed flying fox. For a few months in 1991, unbeknown to the Australian public, news bulletins were delivered with Archie hiding under Morecroft's shirt for warmth. Eventually, it was time for Archie to learn to fly so he could be released back into the wild, but as Morecroft discovered, fostered flying foxes, without parents to demonstrate, don't have the foggiest idea about the adjective they are named for. Morecroft set up flying lessons where he called to Archie from across the room, but Archie didn't budge. Who knows if Morecroft had read Nagel's thoughts on the futility of imagining oneself to have bat wings? Regardless, in desperation, Morecroft began flapping his arms in imitation of flight. Archie was still unresponsive. Eventually, an exasperated Morecroft rested his hands on his hips. Either the arm flapping had taken a moment to sink in, or else Morecroft's pointed elbows and diamond-shaped silhouette in this position were a better approximation of a spread-winged bat, because Archie started flexing his wings and finally made the leap into his first flight.[21] Of course, Archie was a flying fox and not an echolocating microbat, like Nagel's imaginary test case. Perhaps the physical empathy in the relationship between Archie and Morecroft provides more ballast for Jack Pettigrew's 'flying primate' hypothesis?

Donald Griffin, one of the first scientists to discover echolocation in bats, and a specialist in animal consciousness, refers to Nagel's essay as a form of 'paralytic perfectionism', with its defeatist logic discouraging any attempt to step beyond species silos.[22] Such paralysis might be compared to the state Archie found himself in when he couldn't recognize either his own innate batness or Morecroft's attempted portrayal of flight. But Archie took a literal leap of faith; seeing his human carer's arms akimbo, he flung himself across the abyss of species difference and landed on the other side. He may have only landed on Morecroft's head, but metaphorically, he had crossed the interspecies divide. Archie found out what it is like to be a bat by imitating a human imitating a bat. Emily Dickinson took a similar creative leap of faith when, contrary to the tenor of her times, she saw a bat as beneficent, and when, in writing that 'not a song pervades his lips/ Or none perceptible' she intuited something about the physiology of bats that science was yet to prove.

While for Nagel, not knowing is a cause for frustration, others celebrate the collapse of rationality that accompanies genuine engagement with animal subjects. Deleuze and Guattari celebrate werewolves and vampires as the ultimate undoing of humanist pretensions in their chapter on 'Becoming-animal' in *A Thousand Plateaus*; they also refer to themselves as sorcerers. If Nagel had taken his lead from indigenous shamans, his enterprise might have been aided by the ingestion of hallucinogens, as becoming-bat was exactly the condition of the Peruvian shaman Pablo Amaringo after a few too many sessions with the potent hallucinogen ayahuasca:

> And then one night when I was in bed I woke up and realised that I was becoming a bat. My arms were wings. I was screaming and about to fly. When I saw myself like that, a chill went through my body. I said, 'Good Lord, what is happening to me? Am I possessed by the devil?'
>
> Then I got up, and called my mother and my brothers. I told them I was becoming a bat. They said, 'Are you crazy? What are you talking about?' I drank a little bit of liquor and went back to bed.[23]

Australian newsreader Richard Morecroft raised an orphaned flying fox called Archie in the 1990s, and wrote the book *Raising Archie* about his experience.

Depictions of bats from various eras and locations range from delight to abhorrence (and, for the goths among us, delight in the abhorrent). Today, bats occupy a space in the popular imagination that is more potent than ever. Bats have become 'totem' animals to those who crave a symbol to express their difference, to celebrate diversity while ameliorating the pain of being misunderstood. Bat lovers are immediately identified as quirky, existing outside norms, yet their advocacy for bats emphasizes the characteristics that make bats easier to love: bug-eyed babies, maternity, pair bonding and altruism.

Those who are truly enamoured with bats see the world from the same perspective as their chiropteran love-objects, that is, upside down, particularly when it comes to the traditional association of bats with evil. Rather, enthusiasts see bats as leathery-winged angels, while New Agers who co-opt the terminology of Native American spirit animals regard bats as holy messengers. There are those, however, for whom the bat is neither good nor evil but simply one of the family. Deborah Bird Rose, who works with Indigenous Australians from the Northern Territories, notes that these folk see flying foxes as their winged kin and angrily reject injunctions from government officials against touching (or eating) the beings with whom they have shared complex coexistence for thousands of years. There is a sense of interspecies familiarity in the way traditional custodians discuss the habits of their flying family; some stragglers take their time in the nightly fly-outs, or wheel back to the roost because 'those blokes forgot their axes'.[24] Rose refers to 'entangled mutualities', including the relationship of the flying foxes' chattering to the waking up of the Rainbow Serpent, the bringing of rain and the flowering of certain trees at certain times of year. With suitably floral language, Rose calls the pollen-loving flying foxes 'co-evolved myrtaceous mutualists', and for this reason, and many more, the flying fox is a 'keystone' species, for the future of the forest is 'borne on fur and tongue'.[25] The beauty of these 'mutual gifts across species and through time' is sadly lost on those Australians who see flying foxes as noisy, smelly, greedy pests.[26] Rose points out poetic symmetries between Pettigrew's 'flying primate' theory and pre-existing indigenous belief systems.

She wonders if it is our closeness to megabats, rather than our differences, that explains a certain degree of white Australians' hostility towards these creatures: 'I can't help but think that something about them reminds us of us – of how we are when we are at our most crowded, noisy and irritating.'[27] The constant chatter of fruit bats and the silent screams of the echolocaters may be trying to tell us something, as bats are one of the few groups of vertebrate animals that demonstrate vocal learning, and this is a likely precursor to language, that most human of characteristics.[28]

Identification with Chiroptera is literally a matter of perspective. When images of bats wrapped in their wings are turned upside down, they are much more easily anthropomorphized; see for example the photographs of Tim Flach, which capture bats peeking coyly from behind their own 'capes' (*Opera Bat*), gently caressing each other (*Compassion Bats*), or standing stiffly like

Grey-headed flying foxes feeding on eucalyptus blossoms, what Deborah Bird Rose calls 'myrtaceous mutualists'.

Boris Karloff wrapped in mummy's bandages (*Egyptian Bats*). When I look at bats right side up, I see old school rappers in a b-boy stance with arms tightly crossed over their chests, or Clint Eastwood in his signature serape in the 1967 classic *The Good, The Bad and the Ugly*. The change in perspective required by students of bat phenomenology is a useful analogy that enables us to shift out of anthropocentric thinking. 'Perspectivism' is a term used by the Brazilian anthropologist Eduardo Viveiros de Castro to explain an Amerindian philosophy of seeing one's self from the perspective of the other. He also uses the term 'multinaturalism' to describe a worldview in which *all* entities are 'human', possessing their own cultures, and gloriously complicating ideas of 'us' and 'them'.[29]

For some groups who identify with the bat, sexuality is the stand-out quality of this potent totem. The Tzotzil Maya of the Chiapas region of southern Mexico are known as the 'People of the Bat'. Unsurprisingly, post-Conquest, the bat deity that was the symbol of Zinacantán (place of bats) was aligned with the Catholic Devil.[30] Today the 'Black Man of Zinacantán' is a 'black, winged, super-sexed demon' and men will say of a deflowered virgin, 'She was ruined by the bat.'[31] While this all too easily fits the sexual roles imposed by the conquistadores and their church, there may have once existed a more sensuous concept of bat love, intimated by this passage from the books of the seventeenth-century *Chilam Balam* of Yucatán: 'Sweet was the Ancient Fruit and succulent on the tongue; sweet to soften the hard heart; to mollify the angry passions, *Chac Vayah* the bat, he who sucks honey from the flowers.'[32] This casts a different light on the passage from the earlier *Popol Vuh* when Hunahpu loses his head, since Hunahpu also means flower. In this case, Hunahpu's decapitation by a giant bat may be read as overzealous pollination rather than murder,[33] although for the Maya and other Meso-Americans, the assurance of vegetative fertility along with other natural cycles necessitated bloody human sacrifice.

Papua New Guinea is another location in which various peoples identify with a bat totem. Like the Aboriginal Australians who can trace their ancestry back to flying foxes, in the Sepik village of Kandingei a 'Song to the Flying Fox' relates to a time deep in history when men were able to become animals by wearing masks. When they turned into flying foxes they flew away from their women, so the 'Song to the Flying Fox' is the women's lament over their husbands' departure.[34] It is a song raw with the universal agony of rejection: 'You no longer loved your wife/ You no longer liked my sago/ No longer liked my vulva,'[35] and it ends with onomatopoeic weeping. The story is not over, however, as eventually one of the flying foxes crashes into a sago palm, and this turns him back into a man. He is discovered by two sisters who are overjoyed to finally have someone to procreate with, and these offspring become the ancestors of the tribe.[36] So, the tribe is born of a 'failed' flying fox, a clumsy dawdler, like the 'blokes who forgot their axes' in northern Australia. A failed flying fox is also the more 'poetic' evolutionary theory of Jack Pettigrew, the 'fallen angel' theory, in which we were once all flying primates, but some of us unfortunately lost our wings. According to Rose, however, it is the 'blokes who forgot their axes' that play one of the most pivotal roles in seed dispersal, because they are always on the margins of the group, scattering seeds further than the socialites at the centre.

The anthropologist Roy Wagner describes a belief among the Daribi in another part of Papua New Guinea that human beings are not failed flying foxes, but the bats are 'Daribi manqués' because they have lost their genitalia (the Daribi live near a maternity colony and so never see flying foxes with penises). Wagner rather brilliantly describes totemism as a kind of echolocation:

'the reflectivity of differentiating thought proliferating against the landscape of known forms'. In other words, as humans we 'echolocate' ourselves against bats and other animals to build up a picture of our own humanity. Wagner notes that the 'bizarre specializations of the microchiroptera have been most useful in eliciting a human echo'. He asks us to analyse this echo, to figure out 'what kinds of bats are we, and what kinds of human beings are bats?'[37]

For Wagner bats are the 'weirdly altered alter ego' of humans, the 'mammalian stalactites to the human stalagmite'. These mutual inversions infect his language patterns, as in the lovely symmetry of this yin-yang sentence: 'The bat is why we have imagined cave-man; the cave is why we have imagined bat-man.'[38] Wagner postulates that bats and humans are inside-out versions of each other: we reverberate internally and project sound outwards while

The Saisa Peanut Sing-Sing Group from Madang Province, performing at the annual Mount Hagen Cultural Festival in the Highlands of Papua New Guinea.

Tim Flach, *Opera Bat*, 2012.

153

bats reverberate externally; that is, sound bounces back to them. Their picture of the world is the exact inverse of our own; metaphorically speaking, we echolocate off each other.

In Samoa, many men undergo a painful coming-of-age ritual: the imprinting of a traditional tattoo which extends from the hips to the knees. Known as the *pe'a*, which is the name for the native flying fox, it consists of thick black horizontal lines wrapping the male body the same way a bat wraps itself with its dark wings, symbolically sealing and protecting a potential warrior. The tattooing of the *pe'a* is performed today wherever Samoan communities thrive, in the traditional manner, with a serrated bone comb and tapping mallet and all the attendant ritual, including payment in fine mats to the master tattooist or *tufuga ta tatau* (tattoo is a corruption of the Polynesian word *tatau*). It is an excruciating ordeal that can take many weeks to complete. A richly associative text on the *pe'a* was penned by Samoan novelist Albert Wendt, who notes that for some provinces and families, the *pe'a* was a war god, for it possesses a courageous, but also cheeky, nature.[39] Wendt observes that when viewing the *pe'a* frontally, the male genitals look like the head of a flying fox, and the *tatau* spreading out over the thighs resembles bats' membranous wings. Wendt notes pride but also sexual connotations in the expression 'Faalele lau pe'a!', which means 'Let your flying fox fly!' In other words, parade your tattoo for all to see.[40]

It has been noted of Samoan flying foxes that males are easily distinguished from females by their swaying penises, which are so long that they can be mistaken for dangling tails.[41] Such a flagrant display of manhood is perhaps the reason why the bat seemed a suitable totem for warriors and chiefs. Part of the *tatau*, however, is known as *tama'i pea*, the young of the flying fox, which a mother carries under her wings: likewise, the wearer of the *tatau* must protect and nourish his immediate family.[42] One

Greg Semu,
*Self-portrait with
Front of pe'a*, 1995.

154

theory on the protective nature of the *tatau* is that flying foxes are 'well-defended' by their olfactory aura.[43]

Wendt confesses that he himself, for all his honours and tremendous *mana*, does not bear the *pe'a*, and will never do so, lest he have to face the shame of not being able to stand the pain. He says it is far better to remain 'a *pula-u*, a rotten taro like most Samoan males, than be branded a *pe'a-mutu*, a flying fox-that's-been-cut-short'.[44] Yet for all the positive connotations of the *pe'a* in Samoa, one of Wendt's best-known short stories is called 'Flying Fox in a Freedom Tree', a sad tale in which a dwarf has the nickname 'Flying Fox' because, like his namesake, he is an outcast, having 'no nest with other birds because they laugh at him and treat him differently because he is not what a bird should be'.[45] Eventually, he hangs himself in a mango tree, a tragic echo of the real flying fox who hangs in trees and gorges on fruit. For the dwarf, this grisly denouement constitutes freedom, because he was always a 'flying fox with an eagle in the gut' and now he is 'the eagle flying on the mango tree with this one wing of rope'.[46]

Many contemporary Samoan artists have referenced bats or *pe'a* as a way to foreground issues of identity. Greg Semu created a range of self-portraits in which he 'lets his flying fox fly', utilizing both documentary or 'anthropological' style photography and dramatic tableaux. Semu critiques colonial conversion tactics by portraying himself as a Polynesian Christ wrapped in the wings of the *pe'a*, both crucified (2000) and at *The Last Cannibal Supper . . . 'Cause Tomorrow We Become Christians* (2010). The Abrahamic injunction against tattooing the body is here thoroughly flouted, and may have been an influence on the New Zealand cartoon *Bro'Town* created by the comedy group Naked Samoans, in which God himself is portrayed with the *pe'a*; a wonderfully antipodean inversion of angel wings. What would the Master of the Rebel Angels say?

Yuki Kihara, *Tonumaipe'a; How She was Saved By the Bat*, 2004, chromogenic print.

Samoan-Japanese artist Yuki Kihara created a series of self-portraits named *Vavau: Tales of Ancient Samoa* (2004) in which she repurposed the dark grounds and sentimental styling of the black velvet paintings so often exploitative of Pacific female beauties. In *Tonumaipe'a; How She was Saved By the Bat* Kihara portrays Leutogi, a Samoan princess sent to live in Tonga as the second

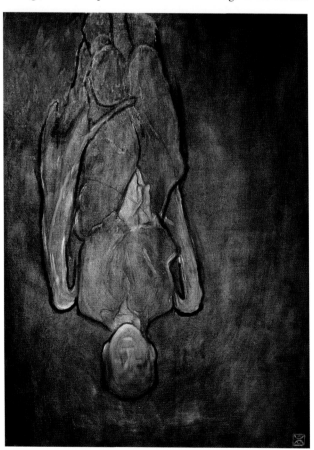

Dan Taulapapa McMullin, *O le Pe'a* (The Bat), 2007.

wife to the king. Isolated and disrespected, Leutogi was further derided when she took pity on an orphaned bat and nursed it back to health. Later, she fell out of favour completely, and was sentenced to death by fire, but the bats remembered her kindness and flocked to her rescue, urinating on the flames. The Tongans then exiled her to a barren island, expecting her to starve to death, but they forgot about her flying fox friends, who flew in fresh fruit for her every meal.[47] Tonumaipe'a, which can be translated as 'salvation comes from the flying fox', is now a chiefly title on the island of Savai'i, and the term *manulagi*, 'bird of heaven', was given to bats in thanks for their preservation of the Samoan line. For a time, they were prohibited food, except to those of high rank.[48] Kihara's portrayal is extraordinarily sensuous: a softly lit Pacific maiden, bound at the wrists, looks beseechingly upwards while bat urine anoints her face like glitter: not in the least repellent, this bat pee is glamorous and magical.

Dan Taulapapa McMullin considers the bat a kind of personal spirit guide, and its form recurs in his paintings, sculptures and poetry. *O le Pe'a* (The Bat, 2007) is a self-portrait of the artist as a young boy, or rather, bat-boy, as he hangs upside down, swathed in soft, sepia-toned leathery wings. The American tabloid the *Weekly World News* created the cult character Bat Boy, whose screaming face and pointy ears sold thousands of issues of the fanciful newspaper. In contrast to that pop parody, McMullin's becoming-bat is far from grotesque sensationalism. Quietly reflective, the washy browns are reminiscent of twilight hush and of strange childish admixtures of fear, wonder and comfort.

McMullin has also written a poem titled 'The Bat', which unlike his eerily pensive painting is a somewhat bawdy, tragicomic tale of Pipi, a *fa'afafine* (Samoan third gender) who is transformed into a bat by the gods and winds up in a cage at the University of Minnesota Medical School.[49] Mirroring the migrations of the artist, who now lives in New York, Pipi the tropical fruit bat finds herself in an alien, snow-covered landscape. She falls in love with a black leather boot left in the snow, and in a case of mistaken identity that McMullin likens to 'falling in love with the oppressor', she becomes stuck to it and dies.[50] But this sticky ending does not discount hope; for McMullin, the bat represents survival, and even though Pipi dies in the Midwestern snows, and Wendt's 'Flying Fox' dies in his 'freedom tree', something of them both survives in the reader.[51]

While McMullin's self-identification with bats is primarily introspective, the social and communicative nature of these creatures is nowhere better illustrated than in the sculpture *Fruit Bats* (1991) by the late Australian Aboriginal artist Lin Onus. In a glorious mix of traditional and contemporary styles, a life-size rotary clothes-line is the roost for a hundred upside-down fruit bats, whose curious faces peek out from bodies wrapped like little mummies in their own wings, painted in the *rarrk* cross-hatch style of bark paintings from central Arnhem Land. Although Onus was a Yorta Yorta man from Victoria, he collaborated with men from Arnhem Land and was given permission to employ the Ganalbingu design for the flying fox in this work.[52] The floor of *Fruit Bats* is littered with droppings, also adorned with the Ganal-bingu flying fox pattern, tying together human creativity and the ability to propagate plants via seed dispersal, while also clearly revelling in the act of mess-making in the hallowed space of the gallery. For those that regard bats as kinfolk, Onus places them firmly in the domestic sphere: *Fruit Bats* is a joyous interspecies integration. For those that insist bats are pests, however, Onus's flying foxes become a phalanx of protesters claiming their land rights in the midst of a white Australian suburban fantasy. The bats send out a clear message: no amount of whitewash will clean this dirty laundry.

Bats recur as insignias of identity and indigeneity across the
Pacific. Dame Robin White, a New Zealand artist of Maori descent,
lived for many years on Kiribati, using natural materials for
her artworks. Her recent installation at the Jean-Marie Tjibaou
Cultural Centre in Noumea featured ten large fruit bats made of
natural bark-cloth fibres, so the bats were pale rather than dark.
White's time spent with women practitioners of various Pacific
fibre arts has endowed her with a wealth of stories, including
the importance of white bats in Tonga and their relationship to

Lin Onus, *Fruit Bats*,
1991.

Dame Robin White
and Ruha Fifita,
*We are the Small
Axe*, 2015.

the Tongan Royal Family. It is said that the appearance of a white bat is an omen signifying the death of a high chief or noble,[53] and for White, these associations with mortality and with sovereignty tie bats to the struggles of the Kanak people in New Caledonia and of Pacific peoples elsewhere.

Pacific connections are also visible in the paintings of Julian Hooper. A New Zealand artist whose Transylvanian ancestor took a Tongan wife, Hooper capitalizes on the Dracula mythos by using a bat as the insignia of Count Gideon Vecsey. In a series of playful watercolours, Hooper fuses magisterial Eastern European tropes with the schematic Tongan heraldry found on *ngatu* – bark-cloth mats – which have also been known to feature geometric bats. Their scalloped wings masquerade as the Count's eye-lashes one minute, the fabric of his wife's skirt the next. Hooper, whose father is an anthropologist, is here creating elaborate kinship diagrams, even depicting his illustrious ancestors in coitus. Bats can be seen as images of fertility: they are fruitful, they multiply and in some paintings they cover the whole surface in pattern, like a tessellation by M. C. Escher, only luminous, colourful and sketchy.

Bats themselves look like such unlikely creations that they are perfect fodder for surreal interpretation. The American painter Tom Knechtel wrote a delightful essay detailing the reasons why bats were worthy subject-matter for art. Echoing the famous proto-Surrealist description of beauty being like 'the chance meeting on a dissecting-table of a sewing-machine and an umbrella',[54] Knechtel suggests the bat is the monstrous result of a 'joint experiment between a botanist and a toymaker' which takes the form of a 'malevolent orchid with balsa wood and tissue paper wings'. Knechtel is amazed that 'anything so eccentric could have found its way past the relentless red pencil of evolution', a phrase equally applicable to the dazzling diversity of Chiroptera and the queer sculptural menageries of American sculptor Tim Hawkinson.[55] Bats are not a frequent subject for Hawkinson; rather, all manner

Julian Hooper, *Sub hoc signo vinces*, from the *Liliu* series, 2007, watercolour on paper.

of odd creatures fashioned from strange materials emerge from his laboratory-like studio. It is no surprise, however, that the creator of a delicate bird skeleton made from his own fingernails would make a couple of creepily mawkish giant bats from twist ties, bread bag tags and plastic bag material.

Black plastic rubbish bags are also the materials used to fashion bat wings by Kathy Holowko, an Australian artist who turned bat making into an opportunity for social engagement and awareness raising. Holowko invited Melbourne's community of bat carers and conservationists to help her decorate two hundred life-sized flying foxes, singeing lacy filigrees into their plastic wings with a soldering iron, so that the light shining through looked like constellations of stars – appropriate to flocks of night fliers. Holowko's *Batmania* hung from the glass ceiling of the Atrium, Federation Square, for a couple of months

in 2015, with a gloriously animated soundtrack of chattering bats. Similarly concerned with Australian flying fox populations, Sydney-based artist Helen Pynor's *The Accidental Primate* (2014) nods to Pettigrew's theories in an extraordinary series of photos depicting individual flying foxes 'blossoming into flight', diving and swooping against a strangely artificial sky.[56] Each bat is juxtaposed with an image of a billowing parachute, as if to underline humans' inability to fly unaided. The natural and the artificial are played off against each other, as the taut bats' wings seem carefully arranged while the parachute possesses a strange organicity. Darker ideas are hinted at – plummeting, collapse, extinction – but whether bats or humanity are the truly endangered species is left open. An Icarus-like fable of folly-in-flight unfolds before our eyes; we are left in free-fall. If Daedalus had modelled his flying paraphernalia on bats rather than birds, his impetuous son would have been

Kathy Holowko, *Batmania,* installation in Federation Square, Melbourne, 2015. Batmania might have been the name for Melbourne, if early colonist (and controversial figure) John Batman had had his way.

wearing wings of leather rather than waxy feathers, and if Icarus had followed the bat's example and flown at night, the sun's rays would never have melted his wings. In aspiring towards transcendence, Daedalus and Icarus forgot whence they came. They forgot, not their axes, but their origins, which is much worse.

Bats are also being celebrated by British artists: Turner nominee Marvin Chetwynd Gaye is known for her carnivalesque performances, yet the most consistent side of her practice is the series of bat paintings she has been working on since 2002 under the collective title *Bat Opera*. While the title might have been inspired by *Die Fledermaus*, the works themselves owe a heavy debt to the swirling skyscapes of the British Romantic master J.M.W. Turner. *Bat Opera* has been turned into a publication: completely text-free, it operates as a kind of outsize flip-book. Without even a title or any visible credits, it compels readers to navigate a language-free

Helen Pynor, *The Accidental Primate 1*, 2014, pigment print on acrylic.

Marvin Chetwynd Gaye, *Bat Opera*, 2013, oil on canvas.

yet strangely narrative realm in which sketchy, painterly bats wing their way through fiery sunsets and dramatic storm clouds. The landscapes these bats preside over are by turns primordial, medieval, industrial and futuristic; there are tornadoes of black bats, murky castles, dark satanic mills and eerie geometric towers. It is a world history (or should that be whirled history?) as witnessed by chiropteran guardians of eternity.

Perhaps the greatest bat-art champion of all, from Britain or elsewhere, is Jeremy Deller. He calls bats Romantic rather than Gothic and his video *Memory Bucket*, a documentary journey through Texas which won him the Turner Prize in 2004, culminates with a powerful sequence of bats streaming out of a cave. Their wingbeats sound like a rainstorm pelting the camera lens: this is the Romantic Sublime, nature at its most awe-inspiring. Deller returned to the bat caves of Texas in 2012 with high-definition 3D filming equipment and made the stunning *Exodus* in which sound, including pitch-altered echolocation, becomes just as important as image. *Exodus* was exhibited as part of Deller's mid-career survey show *Joy in People* at the Hayward Gallery in London, where visitors were given 3D glasses to experience the thrill of being surrounded by bats. Given the exhibition's title, the inclusion of bats seems a little odd. Either Deller finds joy in watching people watch bats, or just possibly he sees bats as people too. And he wouldn't be alone: the Australian bat conservationist Janet Hutchinson calls bats 'really magic people – and I say people advisedly'.[57]

Unlike 'Batsploitation' films which link swarming bats to sinister threat, Deller's documentary-style treatment enables visitors simply to marvel at the magnificent spectacle, which bat conservationist Ted Fleming compares to the mass movements of passenger pigeons and plains bison that were once part of the North American landscape, but have been lost forever.[58] Fleming's fear is that the mass exodus of Brazilian free-tailed bats from Texan caves may also become a thing of the past if we don't fight to protect these natural wonders. Luckily for the bats and for their human admirers, Bat Conservation International have purchased 1,521 acres of land surrounding Bracken Cave in San Antonio to safeguard the area from development.

I was lucky enough to visit Bracken Cave in person, to witness the breathtaking fly-out of 20 million bats at sunset. They are tiny creatures (about 9 cm long) and more like fuzzy moths or tiny swallows, with sickle-shaped wings which en masse create a moiré pattern against the sky. The waves of furred, winged creatures streaming across the sky is like the tide rushing out at the beach, with rivulets of water carving designs in the sand; except that this dazzling patternation is in the sky above, not the waters below, and everything is, as you might expect with bats, topsy turvy. They pour out in unison for what seems like an age, an epoch, a yuga, wave after furry, flickering, fluttering wave.

Deller, having experienced this overwhelming sensation, now does all he can to raise the profile of bats. At the Venice Biennale in 2003, Deller contributed a leaflet to the knowledge-sharing platform 'Utopia Station', outlining the different species of bats found around Venice and their conservation needs. In 2006 he instigated *The Bat House Project*, a public competition to design a functioning bat house on the outskirts of London. In 2012 he initiated *Bats in Space*, a series of evening walks around London with bat detectors and bat experts, so members of the public could better understand the invisible species with which they unknow-ingly share their civic space (perhaps he was hoping that, as Wendy Doniger implies, understanding would lead to love). Deller has even released an album of bat sounds, which, with his famous predilection for acid house and early rave culture, he likens to electronic music.[59]

According to one profile, a Post-it note in Deller's studio bears the legend 'BATS MATTER',[60] and he is constantly asked what it is that he finds so fascinating about these creatures in particular. He replies that we can learn something from bats, since they manage to live together in great numbers in relative peace.[61] Another appropriate response might be: what isn't fascinating about bats? As the poet Maggie Nelson put it when asked why she wanted to write a whole book about the colour blue: 'We don't get to choose what or whom we love.'[62]

As we have seen, bats have been variously associated with sexuality, diversity and sociability, combined with intuition and an ability to navigate through dark places, all of which seem like desirable qualities at the start of the twenty-first century. We are now at a point where we have turned our villains the vampires into sympathetic friends, and our hero Batman into a complicated, flawed individual. Previously reviled, bats and especially baby bats are the latest 'cute' trend on Facebook and other forums where photos and videos proliferate, complete with swaddling cloths, dummies and other pet paraphernalia.

If the days of demonizing the bat are over, perhaps we can revert to Linnaeus' original classification, Pettigrew's primate theories and tribal totemic practices by putting ourselves in the same category as these flying fellows? After all, as warped mirrors of ourselves, they reflect back at us nothing more or less than our own hopes and fears. But coming to this realization requires a certain shift in consciousness, a giving up of old ways, a process for which the bat is itself symbolic. Bats represent to Native American shamans (or at least their self-appointed interpreters) the symbolic death the ego must undertake before exiting the dark

Yo Murata and Jorgen Tandberg, Bat House, Wetlands Centre, London. Project initiated and winning design selected by Jeremy Deller, 2007, project completed 2009.

cave of delusion. The bat becomes symbolic of rebirth because, just as a baby hangs upside down in the birth canal, the bat hangs inverted in the cave, waiting for the right moment to fly out into the world.[63]

Exiting the cave entails a certain amount of fearlessness and a will to adventure that was perfectly exemplified by 'Space Bat', a free-tailed bat that was seen clinging to an external tank during the launch of the NASA space shuttle *Discovery* in 2009. It remains unclear why the bat stayed put, and there was speculation that it had a broken wing. Doubtless, Space Bat went the way of the Russian dog Laika and other animals in space. Yet because Space Bat was a stowaway and not a captive, a mythology of fan art and tribute songs sprang up on the Internet around the brave animal's adventure. While Brazilian free-tailed bats have been documented flying at nearly 3,000 m, Space Bat literally put bats into orbit.[64]

The bat as transformative and transcendent, flying effortlessly from cave to clouds, is exemplified by a Tzotzil folk belief. When a mouse grows old, it goes to a special deserted path, where it attempts to jump four times from one side of the path to the other. If it completes this task successfully, it turns into a bat and flies away.[65] Which brings to mind another Internet meme in which a mouse looks up adoringly at a bat, exclaiming 'Oh my God, an angel!' Indeed, a recent theoretical critique of the role of blood in Christianity postulates that Walter Benjamin's Angel of History, a metaphoric figure based upon a Paul Klee drawing, is in fact a bat, both 'full of love' and 'out for blood'.[66]

But let's get back to the bat cave, because its darkness is nourishing: it represents the blood-enriched womb, not to mention the hearth and home of our ancestors. Sometimes a return to the cave is necessary. Former Australian prime minister Paul Keating once said his speechwriter was 'like a fruit bat' that 'goes back to the dark to feed'. The writer Martin Edmond interprets this colourful observation as a metaphor for research, for 'All writers go back to the dark to feed.'[67] If artists and philosophers, writers and researchers can all count the bat as our totem, let us hope that what we end up excreting sows as many seeds.

When I attended an overnight event monitoring microbats in Melbourne's Royal Botanic Gardens, I scribbled a quotation in my notebook. It was the preface to our induction slide show: 'In the end we will conserve only what we love, we will love only what we understand, and we will understand only what we are taught.' Spoken by the Senegalese forestry engineer Baba Dioum in 1968, these words echo Wendy Doniger's assertion that we only love the animals we understand. Bats may symbolize rebirth, but it is our attitude to bats, and to the natural world in general, that needs to be born again. To us, bats seem inverted, yet it is our attitudes to bats that require inverting. Looking upon bats and their qualities as desirable, not despicable, we might learn to love our reflected selves, as well as the planet we share, all the more. After all, when 'lowly' is said with a Transylvanian accent, it becomes 'lovely'.

Jeremy Deller,
Exodus, 2012. Still
from a 3D digital
video projection.

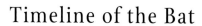

Timeline of the Bat

65 MYA	52 MYA	426–820 CE	c. 1300S	1486–90
Proto-bats evolve from gliding ancestor	*Icaronycteris index* possesses echolocation	Mayan City of Copan flourishes, with the bat as its emblem	Christian demon iconography incorporates bats' wings	Leonardo da Vinci produces sketches of bat-inspired flying machines

1793	1832	1890	1897	1925
Lazzaro Spallanzani discovers that bats can still navigate after being blinded	Charles Darwin witnesses a vampire bat feeding on a horse	Clément Ader claims to have achieved lift-off in his steam-powered bat-shaped aircraft	Bram Stoker publishes *Dracula*	Dr Charles A. Campbell sets up 'municipal bat roosts' in San Antonio, Texas

1982	1986	1989	2006
Ozzy Osbourne bites the head off a live bat on stage; Bat Conservation International founded by Merlin Tuttle	Jack Pettigrew proposes Flying Primate Hypothesis – that megabats are descended from primates	Tim Burton releases his first *Batman* movie: the franchise and logo have been popular ever since	White-nose syndrome emerges as a fatal disease among hibernating bats, spreads like wildfire throughout the U.S. and Canada, killing millions of bats

1554–8	1565	1758	1770
Ancient Maya sacred text *Popol Vuh* is recorded, featuring Kama' Zotz' the 'Death Bat' and a hideous 'House of Bats'	Girolamo Benzoni, journeying through Latin America, writes of bats 'pecking' his hands and feet as he sleeps	In *Systema naturae*, Carl von Linnaeus removes bats from *Aves*, the birds, and puts them into *Mammalia*	A sailor from Cook's *Endeavour* sees an Australian flying fox and thinks it is a devil

1931	1938	1939	1942–4	1974
Dracula is adapted by Hollywood with Bela Lugosi in the lead role	Donald Griffin identifies echolocation in bats	The first *Batman* comic published by DC Comics	Project X-Ray's incendiary 'bat bombs' developed in the U.S. to deploy against Japan	Thomas Nagel writes an essay on the nature of consciousness called 'What Is It Like To Be A Bat?'

2009	2012	2014	2017
Christmas Island pipistrelle becomes extinct	Thousands of fruit bats massacred in a Lebanese cave	Outbreak of Ebola in West Africa, killing 11,000, is blamed on bats (later conjectured); more than 45,000 Australian flying foxes die in a heat wave	White-nose syndrome fungus is found in Texas

References

1 DAZZLING DIVERSITY: THE BIOLOGY OF CHIROPTERA

1 Most publications put the species count at 'over 1,200' but *Bats*, the
   official magazine of Bat Conservation International, wrote in their
   winter 2015 issue that the number was '1331 and counting' (p. 16).
2 Kenneth Chang, 'Primitive Bats Took to the Wing, But They Didn't
   Have That Ping', www.nytimes.com, 14 February 2008.
3 Richard Dawkins, *The Blind Watchmaker* (London, 1998), p. 23.
4 Marianne Moore, 'Poetry', in *Collected Poems* (London, 1951),
   p. 41. In this metapoem about poetry, Moore is arguing that
   intellectualism has outweighed comprehensibility. Aptly, she
   chooses a bat to illustrate the theme of incomprehension.
5 Dianne Ackerman, 'In Praise of Bats', in *The Moon by Whale Light:
   And Other Adventures Among Bats, Penguins, Crocodilians, and Whales*
   (New York, 1991), p. 17.
6 Glover Morrill Allen, *Bats: Biology, Behaviour and Folklore*
   (New York, 2004), p. 142.
7 Comte de Buffon, *Natural History: General and Particular*
   (Edinburgh, 1780–85), pt 4, pp. 323–4.
8 John D. Altringham, *Bats: From Evolution to Conservation*
   (Oxford, 2011), p. 1.
9 Merlin Tuttle, *The Secret Lives of Bats: My Adventures with the World's
   Most Misunderstood Mammals* (Boston, MA, 2015), p. 9.
10 Altringham, *Bats*, p. xiii.
11 Ibid., p. 19.
12 Ibid., p. xii.

13 Graeme O'Neill, 'Batman's Place in Evolution', www.lifescientist.
com.au, 1 February 2008.

14 Ibid.

15 Graeme O'Neill, 'Megabats, Microbats and the Most Interesting
Gene in the Genome', www.lifescientist.com.au, 20 March 2008.

16 Altringham, *Bats*, p. 17.

17 Allen, *Bats*, p. 144.

18 Altringham, *Bats*, p. 10.

19 Ibid., p. 16.

20 Ackerman, 'In Praise of Bats', p. 18.

21 J. D. Pettigrew, 'Wings or Brain? Convergent Evolution in the
Origins of Bats', *Systematic Zoology*, XL (1991), p. 200.

22 Gary F. McCracken, 'Bats in Folklore Part 4: Bats and the
Netherworld', *Bats*, XI/2 (1993), pp. 16–17.

23 Russell Peterson, *Silently, by Night* (London, 1966), p. 51.

24 Allen, *Bats*, p. 64.

25 Henry David Thoreau, *The Journal of Henry David Thoreau*,
vol. XIII: *December 1859 to July 1860* (Salt Lake City, UT, 1984),
pp. 342–3.

26 Ackerman, 'In Praise of Bats', pp. 21–2. The Brazilian free-tailed
bat *Tadarida brasiliensis* is also popularly known as the Mexican
free-tailed bat. I will be following Merlin Tuttle, a global authority
on bats, by referring to this species as the Brazilian free-tailed bat,
including in instances where it was referred to as the Mexican
free-tailed bat in the original text.

27 This peculiar insect became the unlikely subject of a wonderfully
dark children's music video: *Batfly* (dir. Carlos Wedde, 2007).

28 Altringham, *Bats*, p. xii.

29 Donald R. Griffin, *Listening in the Dark: The Acoustic Orientation
of Bats and Men* (New Haven, CT, 1958), p. 5.

30 Matt Soniak, 'Meet the Mariah Carey of Bats', www.theweek.com,
15 August 2014.

31 Ackerman, 'In Praise of Bats', p. 39.

32 Tuttle, *The Secret Lives of Bats*, p. 223.

33 Altringham, *Bats*, p. 14.

34 Charles A. R. Campbell, *Bats, Mosquitoes and Dollars* (Boston, MA, 1925), p. 55.

35 Bill Schutt, *Dark Banquet: Blood and the Curious Lives of Blood-feeding Creatures* (New York, 2008), p. 25.

36 Buffon, *Natural History: General and Particular* (Edinburgh, 1780–85), pt 4, p. 319. A more contemporary take from scientist Bill Schutt acknowledges that the different muscles of bats and birds allow birds a smoother flight style, while bats appear to 'flitter', owing to the simple fact that birds have been flying for a lot longer than bats, see *Dark Banquet*, p. 26.

37 *Superbat* (dir. David Korn-Brzoza, 2004).

38 Griffin, *Listening in the Dark*, p. 5.

39 Altringham, *Bats*, p. 51.

40 John Wenz, 'How Bats Will Inspire the Next Generation of Aircraft', www.popularmechanics.com, 1 May 2015.

41 Leonardo da Vinci, *Notebooks*, selected by Irma A. Richter, ed. Thereza Wells (Oxford, 2008), p. 100.

42 Phil Scott, *The Pioneers of Flight* (Princeton, NJ, 1999), p. 76.

43 Charles Harvard Gibbs-Smith, *Clément Ader: His Flight Claims and His Place in History* (London, 1968), pp. 85, 91.

44 Ronald M. Nowak, *Walker's Bats of the World* (Baltimore, MD, 1994), p. 5.

45 Griffin, *Listening in the Dark*, p. 4.

46 Sue Churchill, *Australian Bats* (Crows Nest, NSW, 2008) p. 23.

47 Emma C. Teeling, Serena Dool and Mark S. Springer, 'Phylogenies, Fossils and Functional Genes: The Evolution of Echolocation in Bats', in *Evolutionary History of Bats*, ed. Gregg F. Gunnell and Nancy B. Simmons (Cambridge, 2012), p. 1.

48 Virginia Morell, 'Holy Blocked Bat Signal! Bats Jam Each Other's Calls', www.sciencemag.org, 6 November 2014.

49 Altringham, *Bats*, p. 64.

50 Ibid., pp. 80–81.

51 Donald R. Griffin, 'Return to the Magic Well: Echolocation Behavior of Bats and Responses of Insect Prey', *BioScience*, LI/7 (2001), pp. 555–6.

52 Ibid.
53 Allen, *Bats*, pp. 135–6.
54 Theodore H. Fleming, *A Bat Man in the Tropics* (Berkeley, CA, 2003), p. 84.
55 Altringham, *Bats*, p. 22.
56 Churchill, *Australian Bats*, p. 24.
57 Ibid., p. xiii.
58 Ibid., p. 88.
59 Brigitte Müller, 'Fruit Bats Are Not "Blind as a Bat"', www.mpg.de, 12 June 2007; Public Library of Science, 'More to Bats' Vision Than Meets the Eye', www.sciencedaily.com, 29 July 2009.
60 Altringham, *Bats*, p. 72.
61 Peterson, *Silently, by Night*, p. viii.
62 Ackerman, 'In Praise of Bats', p. 31.
63 Dawkins, *The Blind Watchmaker*, p. 24.
64 Churchill, *Australian Bats*, p. 21.
65 Tuttle, *The Secret Lives of Bats*, p. 25.
66 This comment was at the Q and A session of 'Battling Extinction: Fighting for our Forgotten Mammals', a film screening at Auckland Zoo, 17 June 2015.
67 University of Auckland, 'Researchers Discover Male Bats Have "Timeshare" Arrangement', www.auckland.ac.nz, 8 June 2015.
68 Altringham, *Bats*, p. 21.
69 Tuttle, *The Secret Lives of Bats*, p. 37.
70 Min Tan et al., 'Fellatio by Fruit Bats Prolongs Copulation Time', www.journals.plos.org, 28 October 2009; Rowan Hooper, 'Bat Fellatio Causes a Scandal in Academia', *New Scientist*, 17 May 2010.
71 Jayabalan Maruthupandian and Ganapathy Marimuthu, 'Cunni-lingus Apparently Increases Duration of Copulation in the Indian Flying Fox, *Pteropus giganteus*', www.journals.plos.org, 27 March 2013.
72 Churchill, *Australian Bats*, pp. 20–21.
73 Tuttle, *The Secret Lives of Bats*, p. 55.
74 Fleming, *Bat Man in the Tropics*, pp. 108, 117. In an earlier article, Fleming posited the number of seeds could be as high as 60,000

per night: Ted Fleming, 'Fruit Bats: Prime Movers of Tropical Seeds', *Bats*, v/3 (1987).

75 Allen, *Bats*, p. 92.
76 Ibid., p. 103.
77 Tuttle, *The Secret Lives of Bats*, p. 66.
78 Altringham, *Bats*, p. 29.
79 Hugh Warwick, *The Beauty in the Beast: Britain's Favourite Creatures and the People Who Love Them* (Oxford, 2013), pp. 44–5.
80 Allen, *Bats*, pp. 98–9.
81 Ralph Rugoff, 'Fluid Mechanics', in *Science is Fiction: The Films of Jean Painlevé*, ed. Andy Masaki Bellows and Marina McDougall (Cambridge, MA, 2000), p. 51. Spelling of 'Quasimoto' in original.
82 Brigitte Berg, 'Contradictory Forces: Jean Painlevé, 1902–1989', ibid., p. 33.
83 Rugoff, 'Fluid Mechanics', p. 50.
84 Ibid., p. 51.
85 Schutt, *Dark Banquet*, pp. 18, 79.
86 Gwen Pearson, 'Bats Have Sparkly Poop', www.wired.com, 30 May 2014.
87 Campbell, *Bats, Mosquitoes and Dollars*, p. 38.
88 Merlin D. Tuttle, 'The Lives of Mexican Free-tailed Bats', *Bats*, xii/3 (1994), pp. 6–14.

2 BATS IN THE BELFRY: MYTHS, MADNESS AND MELANCHOLIA

1 Gary F. McCracken, 'Bats in Folklore, Part 2: Bats in Magic, Potions, and Medicinal Preparations', x/3 (1992), pp. 14–16.
2 Glover Morrill Allen, *Bats: Biology, Behaviour and Folklore* (New York, 2004), p. 20.
3 Gary F. McCracken, 'Bats in Folklore, Part 4: Bats and the Netherworld', *Bats*, xi/2 (1993), pp. 16–17.
4 Steven Connor characterizes flies as archetypal 'anti-angels' – but surely this is the bat's purview? Connor, *Fly* (London, 2006), p. 15.
5 The creature was 'as black as the devil, and had wings; indeed I took it for the devil, or I might easily have catched it, for it crawled very

slowly through the grass'. Francis Ratcliffe, *Flying Fox and Drifting Sand: The Adventures of a Biologist in Australia* (Sydney, 1947), p. 3.

6 Colin Eisner, *Dürer's Animals* (Washington, DC, 1991), p. 98.

7 Francis Bacon, 'Of Suspicion', in *The Essays and Counsels, Civil and Moral* [1625] (London, 1888), p. 187.

8 Gary F. McCracken, 'Bats in Folklore, Part 4: Bats and the Netherworld', *Bats*, XI/2 (1993), pp. 16–17.

9 Ibid. I would argue that having *left* the brain of the unbeliever the bat is not the cause of disbelief, but might in fact be fleeing from it.

10 Rosemary Ellen Guiley, 'Bats', in *The Encyclopedia of Vampires and Werewolves* (New York, 2011), p. 22. There are even more fanciful transformations in the folklore traditions of India and from European gypsies – for whom vampires could become pumpkins, watermelons and household tools. Gary F. McCracken, 'Bats in Folklore, Part 5: Bats and Vampires', XI/3 (1993), pp. 14–15.

11 Girolamo Benzoni, *History of the New World* (London, 1857), vol. XXI, p. 142.

12 Bill Schutt, *Dark Banquet: Blood and the Curious Lives of Blood-feeding Creatures* (New York, 2008), p. 40.

13 Voltaire, *The Works of Voltaire: A Contemporary Version*, trans. William F. Fleming (New York, 1901), p. 145.

14 McCracken, 'Bats and Vampires'.

15 *The Zoology of the Voyage of the HMS Beagle*, under the command of Captain FitzRoy, RN, during the years 1832 to 1836. Part II, *Mammalia*, described by George R. Waterhouse, London (1839), p. 2.

16 They can, however, cause death if they carry the rabies virus, and repeated visits, or team attacks, are enough to polish off a healthy hen in a single night; see Schutt, *Dark Banquet*, p. 4.

17 Bram Stoker, *Dracula* (New York, 1897), p. 141.

18 Ibid., p. 179. Of course, South Sea bats are fruit eaters, and do not attack sleeping men.

19 Ibid., p. 182. I have added my own emphasis to highlight implied racial as well as zoological slurs. Many commentators have pointed out that Dracula can also be read as embodying an irrational fear of the East, with the migrant as a dangerous stranger.

20 Stoker, *Dracula*, pp. 102, 127.

21 Ibid., p. 32. Italics in the original.

22 And brilliantly parodied in the New Zealand mockumentary *What We Do in the Shadows* (dir. Jemaine Clement and Taika Waititi, 2014).

23 Mathew Beresford, *From Demons to Dracula: The Creation of the Modern Vampire Myth* (London, 2008), p. 150.

24 'Bats of a Feather', *The Munsters* (dir. Jerry Paris, 1965).

25 Donald R. Griffin, *Listening in the Dark: The Acoustic Orientation of Bats and Men* (New Haven, CT, 1958), pp. vi–vii.

26 Ackerman, 'In Praise of Bats', p. 40.

27 Kenneth Grant, *Nightside of Eden* (London, 1977), p. 117; ibid., p. 126.

28 *Aesop's Fables: A New Revised Version from Original Sources*, at www.gutenberg.org (2006), p. 100.

29 Comte de Buffon, *Natural History: General and Particular* (Edinburgh, 1780–85), pt 4, p. 318.

30 Lutz Röhrich, 'German Devil Tales and Devil Legends', *Journal of the Folklore Institute*, VII/1 (1970), p. 32.

31 John Ruskin, 'Living Waves', in *Deucalion: Collected Studies of the Lapse of Waves, and Life of Stones* (New York, 1886), vol. II, p. 12.

32 D. H. Lawrence, *The Collected Poems of D. H. Lawrence* (London, 1932), p. 435.

33 Ibid.

34 Ibid., p. 439.

35 Ibid.

36 Ibid., p. 441.

37 Ibid., p. 433.

38 Ibid., p. 434.

39 Hunter S. Thompson, *Fear and Loathing in Las Vegas: A Savage Journey to the Heart of the American Dream* (New York, 1998), p. 3.

40 Ibid., p. 18.

41 James Lipton, *An Exaltation of Larks* (New York, 1993), p. 280.

42 Ibid., p. 35.

43 Tim Pearson, 'No Tree No Me', TedTalks Canberra,
    www.youtube.com, 26 September 2013.
44 Gary F. McCracken, 'Bats in Folklore, Part 1: Bats in Human Hair',
    Bats, x/2 (1992), pp. 15–16.
45 Russell Peterson, *Silently, by Night* (London, 1966), p. 7.
46 Ozzy Osbourne with Chris Ayres, *I am Ozzy* (London, 2009),
    p. 229.
47 Martin Cruz Smith, *Nightwing* (London, 2014), p. 31.
48 Ibid., p. 142.
49 Ibid., p. 66.
50 Ibid., p. 114. Yet again, bats are associated with madness.
51 Ibid., p. 141.
52 *Bats* (dir. John Logan, 1999).
53 Jack Couffer, *Bat Bomb: World War II's Other Secret Weapon*
    (Austin, TX, 1992), p. 81.
54 Ibid., p. 134.
55 Ibid., p. 192.
56 Dennis Tedlock, *Popul Vuh: The Definitive Edition of the Mayan Book
    of the Dawn of Life and the Glories of Gods and Kings* (New York,
    1985), p. 286.
57 Ibid., p. 44.
58 Eric Boot, 'The Bat Sign in Maya Hieroglyphic Writing: Some Notes
    and Suggestions, Based on Examples on Late Classic Ceramics',
    www.mayavase.com, 20 February 2009.
59 Ackerman, 'In Praise of Bats', p. 11.

3 GOOD LUCK CHARM: BRANDED BY THE BAT

1 Russell Peterson, *Silently, by Night* (London, 1966), p. 13.
2 Glover Morrill Allen, *Bats: Biology, Behaviour and Folklore*
   (New York, 2004), p. 31.
3 Ruth M. Boyer, 'A Mescalero Apache Tale: The Bat and the Flood',
   Western Folklore, xxxi/3 (1972), p. 192.
4 Michael Cavendish, ed., *Man, Myth and Magic: An Illustrated
   Encyclopedia of the Supernatural* (New York, 1995), vol. II, p. 205.

5 Catherine Yronwode, 'Mojo Hand and Root Bag', *Hoodoo in Theory and Practice*, www.luckymojo.com, 1 June 2015.

6 Gary F. McCracken, 'Bats in Folklore, Part 3: Bats in Belfries and Other Places', *Bats*, x/4 (1992), pp. 14–16.

7 Ibid.

8 Charles Alfred Speed Williams, *Chinese Symbolism and Art Motifs* (Tokyo, 2006), p. 61.

9 McCracken, 'Bats in Folklore, Part 2'.

10 Allen, *Bats*, p. 27.

11 Ibid., p. 17; Peterson, *Silently, by Night*, p. 5.

12 Boria Sax, *The Mythical Zoo: An Encyclopedia of Animals in World Myth, Legend and Literature* (Santa Barbara, CA, 2001), p. 21.

13 Asia Society, 'Meaning and Decoration in Imperial Ceramics', www.asiasociety.org, 25 January 2005.

14 Ibid.

15 Patricia Bjaaland Welch, *Chinese Art: A Guide to Motifs and Visual Imagery* (Singapore, 2008), pp. 52, 112.

16 Williams, *Chinese Symbolism*, p. 61.

17 Allen, *Bats*, p. 18.

18 Cavendish, *Man, Myth and Magic*, p. 204; Welch, *Chinese Art*, p. 112.

19 Russell Hoban, *The Bat Tattoo* (London, 2002), p. 2.

20 Welch, *Chinese Art*, p. 112.

21 Hoban, *Bat Tattoo*, p. 6.

22 Volker Dürr, *Rainer Maria Rilke: The Poet's Trajectory* (New York, 2006), p. 140.

23 Edward Gorey wrote a picture book called *The Gilded Bat* about imaginary prima ballerina Mirella Splatova, famous for her portrayal of *La Chauve-Souris Dorée*.

24 Paul Louis Couchoud, *Japanese Impressions: With a Note on Confucius* (London, 1921), p. 52.

25 Evelyn Waugh, *Brideshead Revisited* (Ringwood, Victoria, 1984), p. 90.

26 John G. Roberts, *Mitsui: Three Centuries of Japanese Business* (New York, 1989), p. 313.

27 Eric P. Nash, *Manga Kamishibai: The Art of Japanese Paper Theater* (New York, 2009), p. 101.

28 Ibid., p. 143.

29 Ibid., p. 21.

30 Zack Davisson, 'The First Superhero – The Golden Bat?', www.comicsbulletin.com, 19 December 2010. DC Comics' Batman also faces an adversary who is the inverse of himself – Man-Bat, introduced in 1970 but thus far not included in filmic portrayals.

31 Nash, *Manga Kamishibai*, p. 261.

32 Gerald Durrell, *Golden Bats and Pink Pigeons* (Goring by Sea, West Sussex, 2007), p. 96.

33 Gerardo Reichel-Dolmatoff, *Goldwork and Shamanism: An Iconographic Study of the Gold Museum of the Banco de la República, Colombia* (Bogotá, 2005), p. 264.

34 Warwick Bray, 'Gold, Stone, and Ideology: Symbols of Power in the Tairona Tradition of Northern Colombia', in *Gold and Power in Ancient Costa Rica, Panama, and Colombia*, ed. Jeffrey Quilter and John W. Hoopes (Washington, DC, 2003), p. 318.

35 Anne Legast, 'The Bat in Tairona Art: An Under-recognised Species', in *Animals into Art*, ed. Howard Morphy (London, 1989), pp. 270–71.

36 Bray, 'Gold, Stone, and Ideology', p. 320.

37 In the Mix, 'Bacardi: Then and Now', www.inthemix.on-premise.com, 30 June 2012.

38 Maria Poviones-Bishop, 'The Bat and the Guava: Life and Death in the Taino Worldview', www.kislakfoundation.org, 30 July 2001.

39 In the Mix, 'Bacardi: Then and Now'.

40 See 'Heritage: The Bat', www.bacardi.com, 31 March 2015.

41 Ibid.

42 Bacardi Limited, 'Bats Come Home to Roost Near Bacardi Office in South Florida', www.bacardilimited.com, 31 March 2015.

43 Gwen Pearson, 'Tequila, Booze and Bats', www.wired.com, 18 June 2014.

44 Charles A. R. Campbell, *Bats, Mosquitoes and Dollars* (Boston, MA, 1925), p. 3.

45 Bat Conservation International, 'Bats Worth Over $1 Billion to Corn Industry', www.batcon.org, 14 September 2015.

46 Jack Couffer, *Bat Bomb: World War II's Other Secret Weapon* (Austin, TX, 1992), pp. 81–2.

47 Ibid., p. 128.

48 Ibid., p. 6.

49 Ibid., p. 5.

50 Ibid., pp. 118–20.

51 Ibid., p. 61.

52 Ibid., p. 228.

53 Allen, *Bats*, pp. 36–7.

54 Ibid., p. 6. Obsidian in Meso-American cosmology is also related to sharp vision, and this may have further connections with bats' ability to see in the dark.

55 Barbara A. Schmidt-French and Carol A. Butler, *Do Bats Drink Blood? Fascinating Answers to Questions about Bats* (New Brunswick, NJ, 2009), p. 59.

56 J. Hoberman, 'Pop! After Pop!: The Batman TV Show', *Artforum*, LXXXIV/7, p. 249.

57 Carmen Nigro, 'So, Why Do We Call It Gotham, Anyway?', New York Public Library, www.nypl.org, 25 January 2011.

58 Hoberman, 'Pop! After Pop!', p. 249.

59 Ibid., p. 254; Will Brooker, *Batman Unmasked: Analysing a Cultural Icon* (London, 2000), p. 202.

60 Hoberman, 'Pop! After Pop!', p. 250.

61 Gilles Deleuze and Félix Guattari, *A Thousand Plateaus: Capitalism and Schizophrenia* (Minneapolis, MN, 2009), p. 269.

62 Catherine Shoard, 'Dark Knight Rises: Fancy a Capitalist Caped Crusader as Your Superhero?', www.theguardian.com, 17 July 2012.

63 Slavoj Žižek, 'The Politics of Batman', www.newstatesman.com, 23 August 2012.

64 Andrew Ross, 'Ballots, Bullets, or Batmen: Can Cultural Studies Do the Right Thing?', *Screen*, LXII/1 (1990), pp. 26–44.

65 Johann Strauss, *Die Fledermaus* (New York, 2006), p. 85.

66 Dianne Ackerman, 'In Praise of Bats', in *The Moon by Whale Light: And Other Adventures Among Bats, Penguins, Crocodilians, and Whales* (New York, 1991), p. 4.

67 Australian Bat Society, 'Flying Foxes in Melbourne', www.ausbats.org.au, 2 June 2015.

68 As with most colonial foundation myths, it turns out Batman was not such a good guy when it came to his dealings with the original owners of the land. Like the Batman of the comics, John Batman also requires robust political critique.

69 Ibid.

4 THE BELEAGUERED BAT: DEPREDATION, DISEASE AND DEATH

1 John D. Altringham, *Bats: From Evolution to Conservation* (Oxford, 2011), p. 239.

2 Tammy Mildenstein and Carol de Jong, 'Natural History, Ecological and Socio-economic Value of Bats', in *Investigating the Role of Bats in Emerging Zoonoses*, ed. Scott H. Newman (Rome, 2012), p. 23.

3 Roger Croteau, 'Cavern Miners Aim to Gather 200 Tons of Guano', *My San Antonio*, 20 January 2004.

4 Greg Richards and Les Hall, *A Natural History of Australian Bats: Working the Nightshift* (Collingwood, Victoria, 2012), p. 109.

5 Bat Conservation International, 'Can You Guess This Sound?', www.youtube.com, 6 August 2014.

6 Richards and Hall, *A Natural History*, p. 27.

7 Deborah Bird Rose, 'Flying Foxes in Sydney', in *Manifesto for Living in the Anthropocene*, ed. Katherine Gibson, Deborah Bird Rose and Ruth Fincher (Brooklyn, NY, 2015), p. 87.

8 Michael Saunders, 'Helicopters Take Off to Solve Bat Problem', www.townsvillebulletin.com.au, 10 December 2013.

9 Allyson Horn, 'Flying Foxes Return to Queensland Towns in Plague Proportions, as Strapped Councils Watch On', www.abc.net.au, 7 November 2014.

10 Janine Barrett, 'Lyssaviruses', in *Investigating the Role of Bats in Emerging Zoonoses*, p. 80.

11 Erik Stokstad, 'Revenge of the Vampires: Bat Kills Backfiring', www.wired.com, 14 June 2012.

12 Scott H. Newman, 'Significant Zoonotic Diseases Identified in Bats', in *Investigating the Role of Bats in Emerging Zoonoses*, p. 64.

13 Tony Moore, 'Nearly a Third of Bats Now Carry Hendra', www.smh.com.au, 28 July 2011.

14 Newman, 'Significant Zoonotic Diseases', p. 69.

15 Carol de Jong et al., 'Emerging Infectious Diseases', in *Investigating the Role of Bats in Emerging Zoonoses*, p. 4.

16 Merlin Tuttle, 'Merlin's Keynote Message at the 46th Annual Symposium of the North American Society for Bat Research', www.merlintuttle.com, 22 October 2016.

17 Ibid.

18 Craig Smith, Hume Field and Lin-Fa Wan, 'Bat Coronaviruses', in *Investigating the Role of Bats in Emerging Zoonoses*, p. 118.

19 Aizenman, Nurith, '5 Mysteries About Ebola: From Bats to Eyeballs to Blood', www.npr.org, 14 January 2016.

20 Merlin Tuttle, 'UPDATE! Ebola Virus Researchers Considering Alternative Reservoir Hypotheses, Bats Unlikely', www.merlintuttle.com, 24 April 2016.

21 Merlin Tuttle, 'UPDATE! Ebola: Bats Prematurely Blamed', 3 March 2016.

22 Richard Preston, *The Hot Zone* (Sydney, 1994), p. 42.

23 Ibid, p. 43.

24 Ibid, p. 359.

25 Ibid, pp. 366–7.

26 Centers for Disease Control and Prevention, '"Ebola Cousin" Marburg Virus Isolated from African Fruit Bats', www.sciencedaily.com, 2 August 2009.

27 Bat Conservation International, 'Protecting Fruit Bats in Lebanon', www.batcon.org, 12 May 2015.

28 Beth Mole, 'Deadly Coronavirus Found in Bats', www.nature.com, 23 August 2013.

29 Dennis Normile and W. Li, 'Researchers Tie Deadly SARS Virus to Bats', *Science*, CCCIX/5744 (2005), pp. 2154–5.

30 Nadia Drake, 'Why Bats Are Such Good Hosts for Ebola and other Deadly Diseases', www.wired.com, 15 October 2014.

31 Michelle Baker, 'Why Bats Don't Get Sick from the Deadly Diseases They Carry', www.theconversation.com, 23 February 2016.

32 Bat Conservation International, 'The Mysteries of Ebola', *Bats*, xxxiv/1 (2015), p. 11.

33 Michelle Baker, 'Bat's Immunity May Hold Key to Preventing Future Ebola Outbreaks', www.theconversation.com, 16 October 2014.

34 Altringham, *Bats*, p. 254.

35 u.s. Geological Survey, 'White-nose Syndrome', www.nwhc.usgs.gov, 13 March 2015.

36 u.s. Fish and Wildlife Service, 'White Nose Syndrome: A Coordinated Response to the Devastating Bat Disease', www.whitenosesyndrome. org, 31 March 2016.

37 Bat Conservation International, 'White-nose Syndrome Resources', www.batcon.org, 29 April 2015.

38 Bill Schutt, *Dark Banquet: Blood and the Curious Lives of Blood-feeding Creatures* (New York, 2008), pp. 74–5.

39 Stokstad, 'Revenge of the Vampires'.

40 Don't Shoot Bats, 'Keep Australia's Wildlife Safe from Cruelty', www.dontshootbats.com, 15 May 2015.

41 Nick Edards, 'How are Our Politically Problematic Flying Foxes Faring?', www.aqob.com.au, 14 May 2015.

42 Queensland Government, Department of Environment and Heritage Protection, 'Damage Mitigation Permits for Crop Protection', www.ehp.qld.gov.au, 14 June 2015.

43 Tim Pearson, 'No Me No Tree', www.youtube.com, 26 September 2013.

44 Diane Ackerman, 'In Praise of Bats', in *The Moon by Whale Light: And Other Adventures Among Bats, Penguins, Crocodilians, and Whales* (New York, 1991), p. 7.

45 Email correspondence with the author, 25 July 2016.

46 Schutt, *Dark Banquet*, p. 21.

47 Ibid., p. 34.

48 Theodore H. Fleming, *A Bat Man in the Tropics: Chasing El Duende* (Berkeley, CA, 2003), p. 151.

49 Merlin Tuttle, *The Secret Lives of Bats: My Adventures with the World's Most Misunderstood Mammals* (Boston, MA, 2015), p. 64.

50 Fleming, *A Bat Man in the Tropics*, p. 263.

51 Mildenstein and de Jong, 'Natural History', p. 22.

52 Victoria Heywood, *Possum Pie, Beetroot Beer and Lamingtons* (Docklands, Victoria, 2011), p. 134.

53 Ibid.

54 Jean Hewitt, *The New York Times Natural Foods Cookbook* (Melbourne, 1979), p. 38.

55 Mildenstein and de Jong, 'Natural History', p. 22.

56 Katie Moisse, 'A Batty Hypothesis on the Origins of Neurodegenerative Disease Resurfaces', www.scientificamerican.com, 28 May 2010.

57 Altringham, *Bats*, p. 253.

58 Ibid.

59 Hugh Warwick, *The Beauty in the Beast: Britain's Favourite Creatures and the People Who Love Them* (Oxford, 2013), pp. 56–7.

60 Lewis Carroll, *Alice's Adventures in Wonderland and Through the Looking Glass* (Oxford, 1971), p. 11.

61 Justin Welbergen, Carol Booth and John Martin, 'Killer Climate: Tens of Thousands of Flying Foxes Dead in a Day', www.theconversation.com, 25 February 2014.

62 Bat Conservation International, 'Bats and Wind Energy', www.batcon.org, 17 May 2015.

63 Andrew Curry, 'Wind Industry Plans Serious Changes to Protect Bats', www.nationalgeographic.com, 2 September 2015.

64 Fleming, *A Bat Man in the Tropics*, p. 148.

5 POTENT TOTEM: THE BAT IN ART AND PHILOSOPHY

1 Claude Lévi-Strauss, *Totemism* (Boston, MA, 1963), p. 89.

2 Henry David Thoreau, *Walden* (Princeton, NJ, 1971), p. 225.

3 Lévi-Strauss, *Totemism*, p. 78.

4 Hugh Warwick, *The Beauty in the Beast: Britain's Favourite Creatures and the People Who Love Them* (Oxford, 2013), p. 64.

5 John D. Altringham, *Bats: From Evolution to Conservation* (Oxford, 2011), p. xiv; Theodore H. Fleming, *A Bat Man in the Tropics* (Berkeley, CA, 2003), p. 119; Bill Schutt, *Dark Banquet: Blood and the Curious Lives of Blood-feeding Creatures* (New York, 2008), p. 85.

6 Dianne Ackerman, 'In Praise of Bats', in *The Moon by Whale Light: And Other Adventures Among Bats, Penguins, Crocodilians, and Whales* (New York, 1991), p. 54.

7 Schutt, *Dark Banquet*, p. 2.

8 Ibid., pp. 81–2.

9 Glover Morrill Allen, *Bats: Biology, Behaviour and Folklore* (New York, 2004), p. 10.

10 Emily Dickinson, *Complete Poems* (Boston, MA, 1960), p. 653.

11 Sarah K. Donovan and Nicholas P. Richardson, 'Under the Mask: How Any Person Can Become Batman', in *Batman and Philosophy: The Dark Knight of the Soul*, ed. Mark D. White and Robert Arp (Hoboken, NJ, 2008), p. 139.

12 Thomas Nagel, 'What is It Like to Be a Bat?', *Philosophical Review*, LXXXIII/4 (1974), p. 438.

13 J. M. Coetzee et al., *The Lives of Animals* (Princeton, NJ, 1999), p. 35.

14 Ibid., p. 33.

15 Ibid.

16 Ibid., pp. 101–2.

17 Ibid., p. 102.

18 Ibid., p. 439.

19 Ibid., p. 440.

20 Ibid., p. 441.

21 Richard Morecroft, *Raising Archie: The Story of Richard Morecroft and his Flying Fox* (East Roseville, NSW, 1991), pp. 58–61.

22 Donald Griffin, *Animal Minds: Beyond Cognition to Consciousness* (Chicago, IL, 2001), p. 32.

23 Luis Eduardo Luna and Pablo Amaringo, *Ayahuasca Visions: The Religious Iconography of a Peruvian Shaman* (Berkeley, CA, 1991), p. 27.

24 Deborah Bird Rose, 'Flying Fox: Kin, Keystone, Kontaminant',
   Australian Humanities Review, L (2011), p. 122.

25 Deborah Bird Rose, 'Multispecies Knots of Ethical Time',
   Environmental Philosophy, IX/1 (2012), p. 135; ibid., p. 136.

26 Ibid., p. 134.

27 Rose, 'Flying Fox', p. 125.

28 Graeme O'Neill, 'Megabats, Microbats and the Most Interesting
   Gene in the Genome', www.lifescientist.com.au, 20 March 2008.

29 Eduardo Viveiros de Castro, *Cannibal Metaphysics: for a
   Poststructural Anthropology*, trans. and ed. Peter Skafish
   (Minneapolis, MN, 2014).

30 Robert Laughlin, *Mayan Tales from Zinacantan: Dreams and Stories
   from the People of the Bat* (Washington, DC, 1996), p. 2.

31 Sarah C. Blaffer, *The Black Man of Zinacantan: A Central American
   Legend* (Austin, TX, 2012), p. 55; ibid., p. 67.

32 Ibid., p. 119.

33 Ibid., p. 64.

34 Jürg Wassmann, *The Song to the Flying Fox: The Public and Esoteric
   Knowledge of the Important Men of Kandingei about Totemic Songs,
   Names, and Knotted Cords*, trans. Dennis Q. Stephenson
   (Boroko, Papua New Guinea, 1991), p. xx.

35 Ibid., p. 4.

36 Ibid., p. 254.

37 Roy Wagner, *Anthropology of the Subject: Holographic Worldview
   in New Guinea and Its Meaning and Significance for the World of
   Anthropology* (Berkeley, CA, 2001), p. 136.

38 Ibid.

39 Albert Wendt, 'Tatauing the Post-colonial Body', *SPAN: Journal of the
   South Pacific Association for Commonwealth Literature and Language
   Studies*, XLII–III (1996), p. 18.

40 Ibid.

41 Russell Peterson, *Silently, by Night* (London, 1966), p. 120.

42 Wendt, 'Tatauing the Post-colonial Body', p. 22.

43 Alfred Gell, *Wrapping in Images: Tattooing in Polynesia*
   (Oxford, 1993), p. 97.

44 Ibid., p. 26.

45 Albert Wendt, *Flying Fox in a Freedom Tree* (Auckland, 1974), p. 137.

46 Ibid., p. 141. In contrast, Jenny Maclean of Tolga Bat Rescue
    and Research has written an essay called 'The "Devil's Rope":
    Flying-foxes in Barbed Wire Fences' which tells a story, not
    of freedom, but of painful, and fatal, entrapment, in *The Biology
    and Conservation of Australasian Bats*, ed. Bradley Law et al.
    (Mossman, NSW, 2011), pp. 421–3.

47 Patricia Monaghan, *Encyclopedia of Goddesses and Heroines*
    (Novato, CA, 2014), p. 154.

48 Gell, *Wrapping in Images*, p. 98.

49 Dan Taulapapa McMullin, 'The Bat', in *Coconut Milk*
    (Tucson, AZ, 2013), pp. 68–9.

50 Personal communication with the author, 14 May 2016.

51 Ibid.

52 Margo Neale, 'Lin Onus Tribute', www.artlink.com.au, 5 June 2015.

53 Personal communication with the artist, 13 May 2015.

54 Isidore Ducasse, *Lautréamont's Maldoror*, trans. Alexis Lykiard
    (New York, 1970), p. 177.

55 Tom Knechtel, 'Bats', in *M/E/A/N/I/N/G: An Anthology of Artists'
    Writings, Theory, and Criticism*, ed. Susan Bee and Mira Schor
    (London, 2000), p. 347.

56 Ibid., p. 348.

57 Janet Hutchinson, Ku-Ring-Gai Bat Conservation Society,
    'Bat Wraps Episode 2: Totally Smitten – By a Flying Fox',
    www.youtube.com, 24 October 2011.

58 Fleming, *Bat Man in the Tropics*, p. 278.

59 Patrick Barkham, 'Jeremy Deller: I'm More Interested in Ideas than
    Money', www.theguardian.com, 29 January 2012.

60 Charlotte Higgins, 'The Collaborator', www.theguardian.com,
    23 December 2006.

61 Ibid.

62 Maggie Nelson, *Bluets* (Seattle, WA, 2009), p. 5.

63 Scott Alexander King, *Animal Dreaming* (Glen Waverly, Victoria,
    2007), p. 29.

64 Barbara A. Schmidt-French and Carol A. Butler, *Do Bats Drink Blood? Fascinating Answers to Questions about Bats* (New Brunswick, NJ, 2009), p. 14.

65 Blaffer, *Black Man of Zinacantan*, pp. 80–81.

66 Gil Anidjar, *Blood: A Critique of Christianity* (New York, 2014), p. 203.

67 Martin Edmond, 'Riding the Ghost Train', www.booknotes-unbound. org.nz, 10 December 2014.

Bibliography

Ackerman, Dianne, 'In Praise of Bats', in *The Moon by Whale Light: And Other Adventures Among Bats, Penguins, Crocodilians, and Whales* (New York, 1991)

Allen, Glover Morrill, *Bats: Biology, Behaviour and Folklore* (New York, 2004)

Altringham, John D., *Bats: From Evolution to Conservation* (Oxford, 2011)

Campbell, Charles A. R., *Bats, Mosquitoes and Dollars* (Boston, MA, 1925)

Churchill, Sue, *Australian Bats* (Crows Nest, NSW, 2008)

Couffer, Jack, *Bat Bomb: World War II's Other Secret Weapon* (Austin, TX, 1992)

Fleming, Theodore H., *A Bat Man in the Tropics* (Berkeley, CA, 2003)

Griffin, Donald R., *Listening in the Dark: The Acoustic Orientation of Bats and Men* (New Haven, CT, 1958)

Morecroft, Richard, *Raising Archie: The Story of Richard Morecroft and his Flying Fox* (East Roseville, NSW, 1991)

Peterson, Russell, *Silently, by Night* (London, 1966)

Schmidt-French, Barbara A., and Carol A. Butler, *Do Bats Drink Blood? Fascinating Answers to Questions about Bats* (New Brunswick, NJ, 2009)

Schutt, Bill, *Dark Banquet: Blood and the Curious Lives of Blood-feeding Creatures* (New York, 2008)

Tuttle, Merlin, *The Secret Lives Of Bats: My Adventures with the World's Most Misunderstood Mammals* (Boston, MA, 2015)

Associations and Websites

AUSTRALASIAN BAT SOCIETY
ausbats.org.au

BAT CONSERVATION INTERNATIONAL
www.batcon.org

BAT CONSERVATION TRUST
www.bats.org.uk

BAT WORLD SANCTUARY, INC.
https://batworld.org

DON'T SHOOT BATS
www.dontshootbats.com

GIVE A SHIT ABOUT BATS
www.facebook.com/GiveAShitAboutBats.

MERLIN TUTTLE'S BAT CONSERVATION
www.merlintuttle.com

UNEP/EUROBATS
Agreement on the Conservation of Populations of European Bats
www.eurobats.org

Acknowledgements

Many friends have indulged my interest in bats over the years, including Angelique Kasmara, Gwynneth Porter, Allan Smith, Amelia Harris and Alla Sosnovskaia, Brigid Magner, Brett Carroll and their children Augie, Griffin and Violet. Thanks are due to Jacqueline Fahey who encouraged me to paint bats as an undergraduate art student, and much later to Kathryn Tsui, whose enthusiastic curatorial support for a bat-themed solo exhibition in Auckland in 2014 put me in touch with Ben Paris, New Zealand's 'Batman'.

Thanks to *White Fungus* for publishing my first piece on bat love in 2013. Thanks to John Newton for introducing me to Philip Armstrong, author of *Sheep* who encouraged me to get the *Bat* ball rolling, and to Gregory O'Brien for support along the way. Thanks also to the Reaktion team for answering my endless queries, and the wonderful series editor Jonathan Burt for his hospitality, wit and insight.

I'm grateful to friends living near bat colonies who gave me places to stay, and put up with my incessant squeals of delight: Celia Mendoza in San Antonio and Rosemary Forde in Melbourne; and also to those who let me get up close and personal with real live bats: Kate Orgias at the Auckland Zoo, Trish Wimberley at the Australian Bat Clinic on the Gold Coast of Australia, Casey Visintin from Earthwatch's overnight observation of Melbourne's microbats, and artist Kathy Holowko in her Melbourne studio. Valuable suggestions came from Charlotte Craw (who also led me to bat haunts in Cambodia), Michael Mitchell, Geoffrey Roche, Albert Refiti, Robin White. Steve Shimada's echolocations permeated my research, while the wonderfully sharp eyes of Jill Winchester and Kai Jensen made my text presentable, and Caitlin Patane and Amy Parker helped me secure the images to make it sparkle. Edward Colless was a wonderfully supportive boss who encouraged me to use bat research in my teaching – a creative leap of faith in a fine arts curriculum. The Faculty of Fine Arts and Music at the University of Melbourne supported me in paying for a number of the image permissions. Huge thanks goes to all those who permitted me to use their images, especially those kind souls who waived their fees; without their generosity publication would have been impossible. Particular thanks are due to Merlin Tuttle, who not only discounted his incredible photographs, but gave copious advice on bat biology.

The last thank you is also the first and biggest – the initial research and writing of the first draft of *Bat* was assisted by a generous grant from Creative New Zealand.

Photo Acknowledgements

The author and publishers wish to express their thanks to the below sources of illustrative material and/or permission to reproduce it:

Baldwin Library of Historical Children's Literature/ George A. Smathers Libraries/ University of Florida: pp. 13, 14, 81; © 2017 Banco de México Diego Rivera & Frida Kahlo Museums Trust: p. 75; Raymond Barlow: p. 17; Brad Bernard: p. 130; © Eric Cheng: p. 153; © Marvin Chetwynd Gaye/ image courtesy Sadie Coles HQ, London: p. 167; © 1992 Columbia Pictures Industries, Inc. All Rights Reserved/ courtesy of Columbia Pictures: p. 59; © Simon Crowhurst: pp. 28, 31; Paul Cryan/ U.S. Geological Survey: p. 137; Ann Darcy: p. 136; danieljmarsh: p. 36; courtesy Jeremy Deller: p. 65; Jeremy Deller/ The Modern Institute/ Toby Webster Limited, Glasgow: p. 173; © 1999 Destination Film Distribution Company, Inc. All Rights Reserved/ courtesy of Worldwide SPE Acquisitions Inc.: p. 73; Don't Shoot Bats: pp. 113, 127; courtesy Down to Earth Fertilizers, Eugene, Oregon: p. 97; © Linda Evans/ courtesy of the Australian Centre for Egyptology, Macquarie University, Australia: p. 8; © Tim Flach Photography Ltd: p. 152; Folger Digital Image Collection: p. 82; from Ernst Haeckel, *Kunstformen der Natur* (Leipzig, 1904): p. 20; courtesy Tim Hawkinson/ J. Paul Getty Museum: p. 164; Nancy Heaslip/ New York State Department of Environmental Conservation: p. 122; © Helen Hodson: p. 110; Kathy Holowko: p. 165; © Julian Hooper: p. 163; iStock images/ andylid: p. 102 (top and bottom); CraigRJD: p. 6; Vivien Jones: p. 37; courtesy Yuki Kihara/ Gus Fisher Gallery and Milford Galleries Dunedin, New Zealand: p. 156; from W. F. Kirby, *Natural History of the*

Readers are free:

- to share – to copy, distribute and transmit the work
- to remix – to adapt the this image alone

Under the following conditions:

- attribution – You must attribute the work in the manner specified by the author or licensor (but not in any way that suggests that they endorse you or your use of the work).
- share alike – If you alter, transform, or build upon this work, you may distribute the resulting work only under the same or similar license to this one.

Index

Page numbers in *italics* refer to illustrations